techniques for
machine-embroidered design

That
Patchwork
Place®

Quilted Sea Tapestries

ginny
eckley

QUILTED SEA TAPESTRIES:
Techniques for Machine-Embroidered Design

© 1995 by Ginny Eckley

That Patchwork Place, Inc.,
PO Box 118, Bothell, WA 98041-0118 USA

Printed in Hong Kong
00 99 98 97 96 95   6 5 4 3 2 1

Library of Congress Cataloging-in-Publication Data

Eckley, Ginny,
Quilted sea tapestries : techniques for
machine-embroidered design / Ginny Eckley.
p.   cm.
ISBN 1-56477-083-4 (pbk.)
1. Embroidery, Machine. 2. Quilting.
3. Sea in art. I. Title.
TT773.E35   1995   94-42688
746.44'028—dc20   CIP

credits

Editor-in-Chief .... Barbara Weiland

Technical Editor .... Kerry I. Hoffman

Managing Editor .... Greg Sharp

Copy Editor .... Liz McGehee

Proofreader .... Leslie Phillips

Illustrator .... Brian Metz

Illustration Assistant .... Lisa McKenney

Photographer .... Brent Kane

Design Director .... Judy Petry

Cover and Text Designer .... David Chrisman

Production Assistant .... Claudia L'Heureux, Shean Bemis

MISSION STATEMENT

WE ARE DEDICATED TO PROVIDING QUALITY PRODUCTS
THAT ENCOURAGE CREATIVITY AND PROMOTE SELF-
ESTEEM IN OUR CUSTOMERS AND OUR EMPLOYEES.

WE STRIVE TO MAKE A DIFFERENCE IN THE LIVES
WE TOUCH.

That Patchwork Place is an employee-owned, financially secure company.

acknowledgments

My heartfelt thanks to:

All who take the time to appreciate the beauty and uniqueness of art;

All the photographers and writers who have provided me with magnificent material;

The divers who have seen the underwater life and shared their knowledge;

The manufacturers who have provided me with high-quality products to work with—Pellon, Bernina, Schmetz, Mettler, and Rowenta.

*T*able of contents

dedication

The sewing bug bit me at an early age. Thanks to my mother, Harriet Murnane, and her mother, Hattie Gillivan, for passing on the gift of patience. My father watched amusingly as I made things he did not comprehend, and fortunately, he learned when not to say anything! I thank him for passing on persistence and strength of character.

I came from a strong, supportive family and had the good fortune of marrying into one. My husband, Ty, dreams big and can envision more than anyone I know. I thank him for pushing me to achieve at a higher level. Thanks to my children, Amber and Forest, who are developing talents of their own. My mother-in-law, Anne Eckley, is an artist who has always been generous and continually encouraged me to create. I admire my father-in-law, Gerry Eckley. He has been influential in setting an example of perseverance and generosity. And to all my brothers and sisters, friends, teachers, clients, and fellow artists who have encouraged me along the way, thank you!

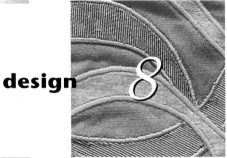

Introduction

I have always had the compulsion to make things. As a little girl, I made Troll doll clothes and spent my spare time at the local hobby shop. I started making my own clothes at the age of twelve and continued sewing through college. I enrolled in every sewing class available, including various classes in fiber sculpture and weaving.

Upon completing several art courses, I switched my major, ultimately graduating with a Fine Arts degree from the University of Houston. After graduating, I worked with a designer, making custom clothing and accessories. I also took classes in art glass. Different colors of glass combined with light fascinate me. Although fabric and glass seem worlds apart, I continue to create art in both mediums. Each has its design limitations, and each provides unique artistic opportunities.

Glass is rigid, yet through etching, I can draw images and create depth through shading and carving. Glass comes in so many colors and textures and can be transparent or opaque.

For an artist, this allows a limitless source of design possibilities. Through my glass commissions, I have been able to explore the pleasures and limits of the glass medium.

My sea tapestries have evolved as a study of nature and a love of fabric. The colors of fish captivate me. After researching their habitats, I became enthralled with the life that exists under water. Snorkeling, aquariums, tide pools, and numerous books and magazines have kept my interest alive. With each tapestry, I learn about another creature and its fragile environment. At the same time, I explore possibilities that only fabric and thread can provide. I continually strive to bring knowledge and beauty to others through my work.

This book covers techniques that work for me and the machine that I use. It is not necessary for you to have the latest computerized sewing machine to achieve wonderful results. It is important for you to know your machine and to feel comfortable using it. Your machine must be in good working order and capable of doing zigzag stitches. It is also helpful to be able to shift the feed dogs up and down.

Loosen up, have fun, and enjoy the process of exploring these techniques while stitching a new creation.

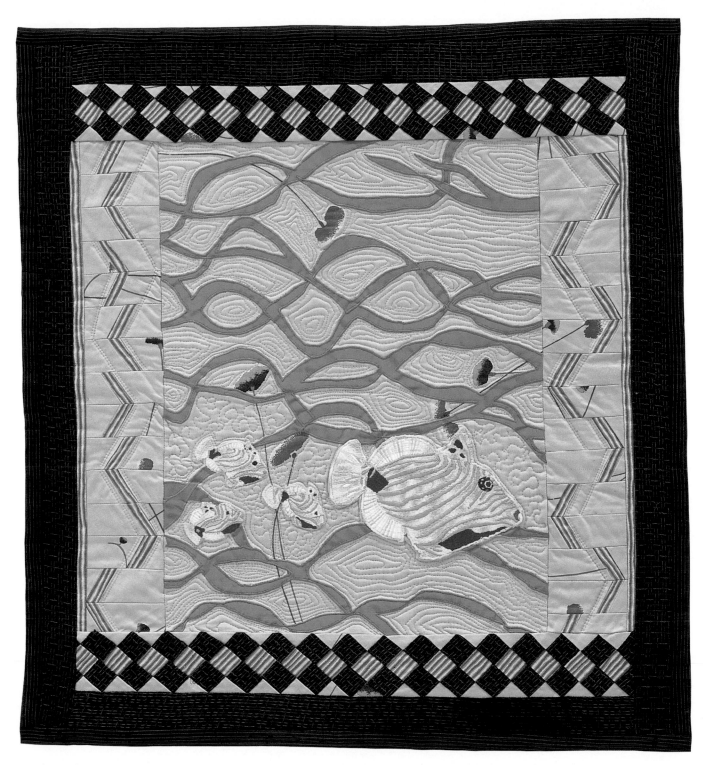

UNDULATED TRIGGERFISH [22½" x 24"]

A mother triggerfish leads as three baby fish playfully follow. Water reflections inspired the deep blue appliquéd shapes. Seminole piecing finishes the borders.

Design

I begin my sea tapestries by looking through my library of books and magazines on fish. Usually a particular fish will fascinate me, and I will design a piece around it. I research and discover all I can about that fish, its habitat, size, and other fish that are compatible or incompatible with it. Once my mind is full of facts, I start drawing. Most often, my finished piece doesn't end up like my original designs, but to me, it is all part of the process. Each step along the way adds an idea to the final work.

Two tools that I love to use for design are the copy machine and the computer. I enlarge, reduce, rotate, reverse, and make multiples of the fish. I make paper patterns of the fish in a variety of sizes and views. Usually, I draw more than one view so that a school of fish will appear realistic.

The drawing stage is very much an experimental stage. I try everything that might possibly work. Note the variety of ways I have drawn the parrotfish and the notes I added pertaining to color, habitat, or the book where I found the fish.

Often, I have an idea and am not sure if it will work, so I test the idea out on the sewing machine before completing my design.

Once I have drawn the fish that I want to use in my design, I color the fish drawing. Using the techniques described in the machine-embroidery section, beginning on page 20, I draw the design onto interfacing with a pencil. At this point, I machine embroider the fish, using the colored drawing as my guide.

After the fish are stitched, I start pulling out fabrics that complement them. See pages 10–14 for details on how I select fabrics for my tapestries.

Getting stuck in a composition is normal. Here are a few tips to help you find a solution.

✦ It helps to tack your work up on a wall or on a foam-core board and stand away from it as far as you can. You want to read your piece close up and from a distance. Try placing a variety of fabrics next to your work. Often, two fabrics next to each other create a spark of magic.

✦ Go back to your original drawings. Pull out the book or article that inspired you in the first place. Often, we have so many possibilities in front of us, we become overwhelmed. Work on a part of the piece that you are sure of, then go back to the challenging spot.

✦ Threaten yourself! If you don't find a solution, you have to clean your studio. Sounds crazy, but while I'm tidying up, I'll pick up fabrics and often find a solution. Also, cleaning or reorganizing sometimes clears the way for new thoughts.

✦ Look at other artists' work. Analyze artwork that you find stimulating, asking yourself how they designed and balanced their compositions. Try to imagine their work in black and white, because color is sometimes distracting when you are analyzing a composition.

✦ When you start to draw, you have a new way of looking at things—you really see them. Take a walk outside and appreciate nature. One of my favorite places to run is by a lake where I often see egrets and herons. The beauty of the place and the birds always amazes me. I come home feeling uplifted and ready to work.

With each tapestry, I challenge myself to try a new technique or two. It keeps my work fresh, and I usually end up with more ideas for the next piece.

What if you aren't crazy about fish but love birds or flowers? Research, design, draw, and stitch—the same process applies whether you want to create fish or fowl! Let your imagination go!

My early sketches and sources of inspiration for the "Rainbow Parrotfish" tapestry.

Fabrics and essentials

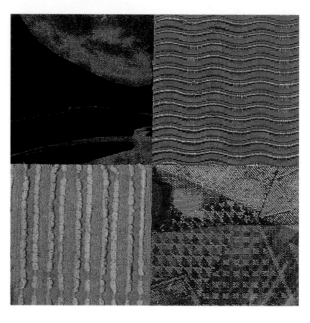

fabric overview

What I love about my fish tapestries is that I can use every type of fabric imaginable. Interior decorator fabrics offer a world of possibilities. Many decorator fabrics are too heavy for clothing but are perfect for artwork. You can find very abstract and contemporary designs, many of which are hand-painted or silk-screened. Also, most decorating fabrics are 54" to 60" wide, making them useful for large tapestries or quilts.

After I have designed my tapestry and made the fish, I select the fabrics, starting with the background. Then I work forward, adding layers of details. My fabrics are sorted by color, making it easy to pull fabrics. I have separate containers for tapestry fabrics and fabrics that I plan to use for clothing. When I am designing, my sewing room looks like a cyclone has hit!

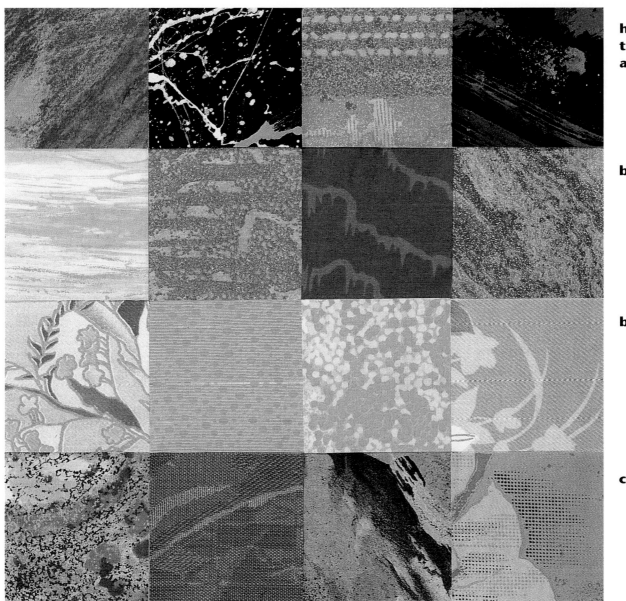

handpainted, textured, abstract

background

blending

contrasting

My favorite fabrics are hand-painted designer fabrics that I purchase in interior decorating shops and design showrooms. Ones that are abstract and have texture work well for me. I also love to use both blending and contrasting fabrics. The compatible fabrics allow the design to flow, while the contrast gives it life and interest.

I collect textiles from fabric, quilting, and decorator stores. Decorator fabrics are usually of a heavier weight, which supports many layers of appliqué. They also hold up well during machine-embroidery stitching. Another advantage is that the prints in the decorator fabrics tend to be larger and appear more exotic.

A great way to achieve depth and shading is to purchase a fabric in a variety of colorways (the same print in different colors).

I also like velvets, tulles, silks, and other "fancy" fabrics that can be found in stores specializing in costume-making supplies.

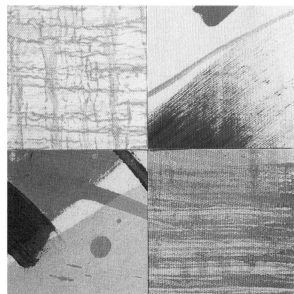

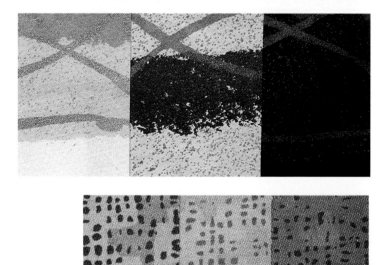

Another source of unique fabrics are shops that sell bridal fabrics. Look in the netting and tulle section. One of my favorite effects is to use a variegated tulle to cover and darken an area, which creates an illusion of depth and shadow.

Flocked tulle and tulle with small bits of glitter are also available. They can add just the right sparkle to water or create reflections of light on fish.

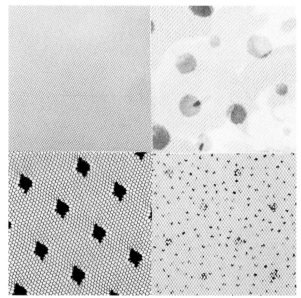

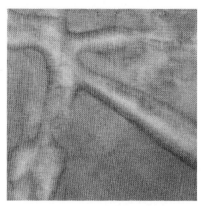

If you can't find tulle, look at sheer fabrics. I've found unusual dye patterns, and if they are sheer enough, they give an effect similar to tulle.

There are times when you feel you have the right fabric, but the color is a little off. In these situations, try fabric markers to change the color. Another easy option is to use fabric paint and sponge the paint on. In the pink fabric of the "Sea Anemones" tapestry on page 36, the turquoise and white paint have been sponged on to give the fabric more texture.

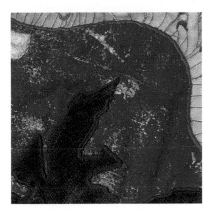

Even though I have hundreds of fabric choices, I still like to dye fabric. Since my idea of dyeing is to create variety, I always dye several pieces of fabric at once. Some printed fabrics do not accept the dye evenly, creating new color patterns. If the pattern in the fabric is overprinted with a different dye or textile paint, the dye you are using will usually dye the background fabric but may not penetrate the overprinted areas. There are a number of dye products on the market—follow the manufacturer's directions and experiment to find the ones you like best. Part of the joy of dyeing is the surprise that usually comes with the results.

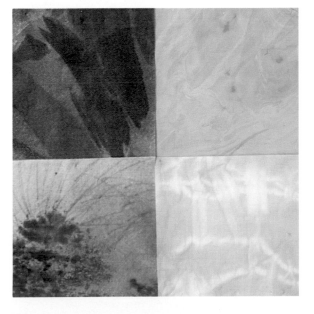

TIP: Before dyeing, wash and machine-dry your fabric to remove sizing and fabric protectors. Before you remove the fabric from the dye pot, remember that the fabric will be lighter after it has dried. Leave it in the dye pot until it looks a shade darker than the color you want.

Clothing is also one of my fabric resources. They may go out of style, but sometimes the

fabric in a dress or accessory is so nice I can't throw it out. In the "Trunkfish" tapestry, the brown coral is made with leather from a purse.

Do not rule out thrift stores as a source of wonderful fabrics. Look for things that are in good condition. You can never have too many fabrics in your collection. Having a wide section of fabrics means, when an idea comes to you, you can jump right in!

The little blue fish in the "Filefish" tapestry are from blue jeans, and the velvet border in "Andaman Island" is from a pair of slacks.

I encourage you to machine quilt on cotton velvet. Rayon velvet is "wiggly" and tends to shift as you sew. The "Clown Triggerfish" tapestry on page 49 has a narrow, striped velvet in the background. After this project was machine quilted, the stripes were broken up and the pattern became more wavelike. The tapestry has an intangible rich appearance that draws people in to get a closer look.

Often, I use only parts of a fabric. Study your fabrics to see what lines, colors, motifs, and designs are included in the overall piece. As in many appliqué projects, sometimes a splash of color, the color of a leaf, or a petal of a flower will be exactly what you want. Be open to using sections of your fabric. In the fabric below, I chose to use only the background, not any of the design motifs.

For large background pieces, it is best to cut the fabric with the grain. With appliqué pieces

that are 7" or smaller, I cut the fabric according to what looks best with my design, disregarding the grain lines.

When cutting borders, I prefer to cut on the straight of grain. Either crosswise or lengthwise will work, but you need to be consistent. Bias strips tend to stretch and ripple, so avoid using them for borders.

When working with fabric, part of the challenge is to discover its potential and the many ways to manipulate it.

interfacings, stabilizers, fleece, and fusible web

When I create a fish completely with machine embroidery, I make a sandwich of fusible interfacing, fleece, and tear-away stabilizer. I draw the design directly onto the interfacing. I prefer to use Craft-Bond™ by Pellon® because it is sturdy and holds up during all of the stitching. If it is not available, choose an unwoven, heavyweight, white fusible interfacing.

The middle layer is fleece. In fabric shops, fleece is usually displayed next to the interfacings. I use Thermolam® by Pellon and Pellon Fleece (#988, a lofty polyester fleece). Both of these are 45" wide and are sold by the yard.

Below the fleece, I add a layer of tear-away stabilizer. My favorite is Stitch-n-Tear® by Pellon®. Other brands are fine, but choose the heaviest weight available.

For appliqué, I like to use Pellon Wonder-Under® Transfer Web. It comes in two weights—light and heavy. If the fabric you are using is as heavy as denim, use the heavy weight. Sometimes I use HeatnBond™ and Stitch Witchery®, or Aleene's. Use those that have a paper backing you can draw on. Note the heat settings recommended by the manufacturer and use a press cloth.

HARLEQUIN TUSKFISH [21" x 23"]

Sea kelp sways over two male tuskfish, who bare their teeth as they prepare to fight. A third tuskfish watches intently, partially hidden amid the coral.

Threads and needles

There are so many thread choices, not only of color but of weight and fiber content. Choose thread from reputable manufacturers. Bargain bins may give you a thread that breaks so often you'll want to give up! Look at the weight and fiber content before you buy. The smaller the number, the finer the thread. If there is a second number, it refers to the ply. Ply is a strand in thread or yarn that has two or more strands twisted together for strength. So 60/2 is 60-weight and 2-ply. My advice is to try several types to find what you like. Experiment! The following threads are suitable for machine embroidery.

Cotton thread is one of my favorites. It is a fine, 2-ply thread with a luster that is compatible with most fabrics. Cotton 30-weight thread is extra fine and great for detail areas, such as the eye of a fish. The most commonly used thread for satin stitching is 60-weight. I like to use it to fill in areas. Since it is made from short fibers, lint collects quickly under the throat (needle) plate and around the bobbin case and feed dogs. Be sure to clean these areas often as you sew.

Metallic threads have improved since they were first introduced, but try to use the top-quality brands. Check the end of the thread to see how it unravels. Make note of the weight. The finer metallic threads with a small ply number are easier to work with. If you find it unraveling as you sew, switch to a needle with a bigger eye, such as size 90/14.

Thicker metallic threads can still be used, but instead of threading them through the needle, lay them on top of the fabric and use fine nylon thread and small zigzag stitches to tack (or couch) them down.

Rayon thread comes in a beautiful array of vibrant colors. It is helpful to use a thread net over the spool to prevent tangling.

Silk thread has a shiny luster and is the only natural thread that is a continuous filament. It is a pleasure to sew with but is also expensive.

There are many variegated threads available. Some incorporate the whole color spectrum and can dominate a piece. For the fish tapestries, I prefer a cotton that has many hues of one color. It creates depth and shading without having to change the thread. Look for ones that change colors slowly, blending colors together.

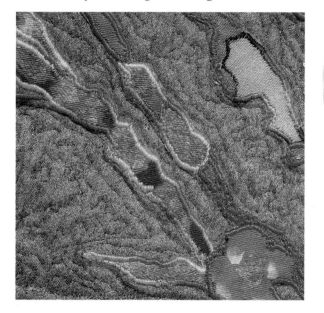

Nylon thread is what I use to do the final machine quilting. Only the fine, thin .004 gauge will work. Two brand names of this gauge are Wonder and Stitch Thru, available in most quilt stores. They come in clear for light-colored fabrics, and smoky gray for dark fabrics.

Cotton basting thread is used in the bobbin for appliqué, machine embroidery, and machine quilting. It usually comes on a large-size spool and is 50-weight. A brand I like is Brooks basting thread by J. & P. Coats®. It is often found in white or black. If it is not available, use cotton embroidery thread in the bobbin.

I have found that it is important to have on hand extra needles that work with the threads you are using. Nothing is more frustrating than to have skipped stitches, or to have threads break because the needle is not compatible with the thread. The following chart gives my recommendations for needles and thread. Always test the needle on a scrap of the fabric you will be stitching on to make sure it doesn't put holes in the fabric.

THREAD	NEEDLES
Metallic	80/12
	90/14 embroidery
	90/14 topstitch
	90/14 metafil
Rayon	90/14
Silk	80/12
Cotton (light-medium fabric)	80/12
Cotton (heavy fabric)	100/16 (Schmetz Jean/Denim)

If the thread breaks frequently, switch to a needle that is one size larger.

OCEAN SURGEONFISH [19" x 24"]

A school of blue surgeonfish swim among multicolored coral. Seminole piecing finishes the upper and lower borders.

QUEEN PARROTFISH IN A CORAL JUNGLE [24" x 29"]

The parrotfish has very sharp teeth, capable of eating coral. Chamois leather is a good choice for the coral in the foreground, and machine embroidery highlights the purple sponges and variegated gray algae. Light gray Bermuda chub swim behind the coral mass. Variegated thread and a strip of appliquéd waves unite the background with the bright foreground. Seminole piecing finishes the upper and lower borders.

Machine embroidery

Free-motion machine embroidery often strikes fear in otherwise confident needleworkers, seamstresses, and fiber artists. Like hand embroidery, the more you practice, the more relaxed you'll be. As you gain confidence, you will develop other ideas and discover the endless possibilities that machine embroidery has to offer. Try the techniques in this book and have fun!

materials

- ✦ 9" or 10" adjustable embroidery hoop (wood or plastic)
- ✦ 1 yd. medium to heavyweight white, nonwoven interfacing, such as Craft Bond
- ✦ 1 yd. fleece, such as Thermolam
- ✦ 1 yd. tear-away stabilizer
- ✦ Variety of machine-embroidery threads*
- ✦ Size 80/12 or 90/14 machine-embroidery needles (Sharps, not ball-point)
- ✦ #2 pencils
- ✦ Sharp embroidery scissors
- ✦ Lightweight cotton press cloth and iron

Cotton threads are preferable; variegated cotton threads are beautiful and instantly create shading and depth.

embroidery hoops

Embroidery hoops come in a variety of shapes and materials. They are made of plastic, wood, or metal. Many of the plastic hoops have a spring-loaded metal inner ring that fits in a groove in the plastic outer ring. Wood and some plastic hoops have a screw on the outer ring that adjusts the hoop for varying tensions and fabric widths. I have found that the spring-loaded plastic hoops work best with finer fabrics, such as silks and delicate cottons. The wood hoops work best for heavier cotton and decorator fabrics.

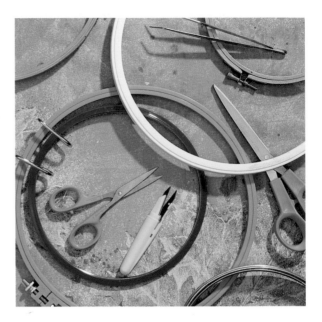

embroidery hoop setup

1. Cut a square of interfacing 2" larger than your embroidery hoop. If your hoop is 10", cut a 12" square.

2. Using the practice fish pattern on page 81, center the pattern under the interfacing and trace the pattern onto the right side of the interfacing with a pencil. Be sure to trace the wave lines as well.

> **TIP:** Always test pens and markers on a scrap of the fabric that you will be marking on. Pens and markers sometimes bleed when ironed.

3. Cut the same size squares from the fleece and the tear-away stabilizer.

4. Using the press cloth, fuse the interfacing to the fleece.

5. Place the tear-away stabilizer on the other side of the fleece. Baste the three layers together to make a "sandwich."

6. Loosen the screw on the larger ring of the hoop. Lay the hoop flat on a table, with the screw side facing toward you.

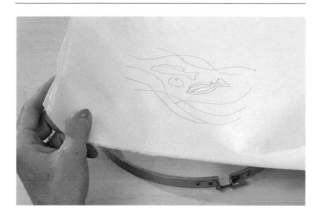

7. Place interfacing with traced fish design face up on top of the ring.

8. Insert the smaller hoop ring on top and tighten the screw. Pull the fabric layers around the edges to tighten. Gently push the smaller ring

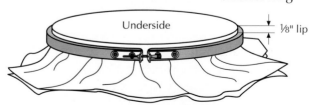

inside the outer ring so that the underside extends beyond the outer ring approximately $1/8$". This lip makes it tighter and allows the hoop to move more freely across the throat plate of the machine. Tighten the screw.

9. Leaving 1" of fabric outside of the hoop, trim the corners of the layered fabric. This makes it easier to work with.

adjusting the sewing machine

The most important tool in this art form is your sewing machine. Take the time to clean and oil your machine. Remove the throat plate and brush the lint from the feed dogs.

Now that your machine is cleaned and oiled, set the tension. I know that the word tension can bring fear to the bravest machine operator, but once you understand a few basics, your fear will vanish!

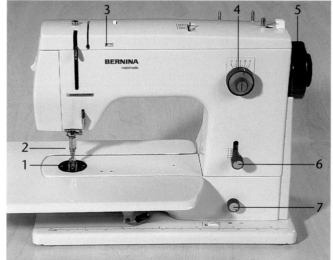

1. Throat plate
2. Presser foot
3. Top tension indicator
4. Zigzag adjusting knob
5. Handwheel
6. Stitch length adjustment
7. Feed dogs control

machine embroidery

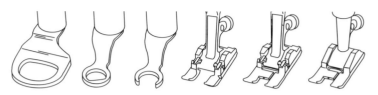

Machine-Embroidery Feet

First, adjust the bobbin tension. A basic rule to remember is: left to loosen and right to tighten. Slightly loosen the bobbin tension. A small screw on the outside of the bobbin case regulates the tension.

Left to loosen   Right to tighten
Bobbin Tension Adjustment

When the screw is loosened, more space is allowed for the thread to pull through. It usually takes only a quarter of a turn to adequately loosen the bobbin tension. Wind a bobbin with cotton basting thread to practice adjusting the tension. Thread the bobbin, and as you pull the thread, it should feel firm but not tight. If it feels tight, turn the screw to the left to loosen. If your bobbin case has numbers on it, adjust to a smaller number. Insert the bobbin case into the machine.

Next, adjust the upper tension. With machine embroidery, the upper tension is much looser than the lower tension. This causes the upper thread to make raised stitches. You will see the upper thread on the underside of your work, along with the bobbin thread. If you are making a wide zigzag stitch, the upper thread will be on both sides of the bobbin thread, on the underside of your work.

Reduce the upper tension by one full number to start. As you sew, you can make further adjustments if necessary.

TIP: I have found it convenient to have an extra bobbin case set at a looser tension. My other bobbin case is set at a normal tension.

a note about feed dogs

Each sewing machine varies, but when I am doing appliqué, I generally keep the feed dogs up. If your fabric is not moving as freely as you would like, or if the stitches are too small, lower the feed dogs and test the movement on a scrap of your fabric. Be sure to check the underside of your work because sometimes loops of thread are created.

I lower the feed dogs when I do free-motion embroidery, make machine lace, and when I machine quilt through many layers of fabric.

machine setup

1. Remove the presser foot and needle; lower the feed dogs.

2. Set your stitch width at a medium zigzag. The stitch length is controlled by the movement of the hoop.

3. Place the hoop on the throat plate of the machine.

4. Insert a new needle. A size 80/12 or 90/14 Sharp is best, not a ball-point needle.

5. Insert a darning foot or a free-motion embroidery foot.

6. Lower the presser foot.

7. Thread the top of the machine with a brightly colored embroidery thread. Use basting thread in the bobbin. If you cannot find basting thread, use embroidery thread.

machine embroidery

8. Stitch the circle first. Line up your hoop so that the X in the circle is under your needle.

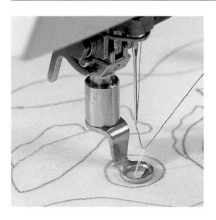

9. Lower the needle into the X. Bring the bobbin thread to the top surface by holding the top thread and turning the handwheel.

With both threads on top, hold them taut and stitch in place to lock the threads. Clip threads. Make sure the presser foot is down or you will get a mass of loops underneath your work.

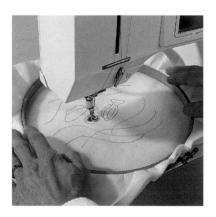

10. Place your hands on the sides of the hoop and relax! Glide the hoop from side to side until the circle is filled. Use wider stitches to fill the circle and narrower stitches around the perimeter.

11. When you have finished stitching, set the stitch width at 0 and take 2 to 3 stitches to knot. Clip only the top thread; the bobbin thread does not have to be cut until you are ready to remove the hoop.

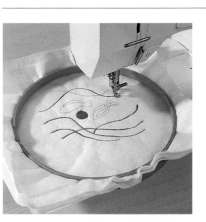

12. Next, practice some of the wave lines. Vary your stitch widths from 0 to as wide as your machine will go. Try to move at an even, moderate speed. Remember to relax and think of this as doodling!

TIP: You will notice from experimenting that the wide stitch width fills the area faster, but because the stitch takes such a big bite, it is harder to control. It is best used in large areas.

If the edges are not as even and controlled as you would like, go around the outer edge slowly, using a small zigzag stitch.

13. Change to a different thread color—use a variegated thread if you have one!

14. With a small zigzag stitch, outline Fish #1.

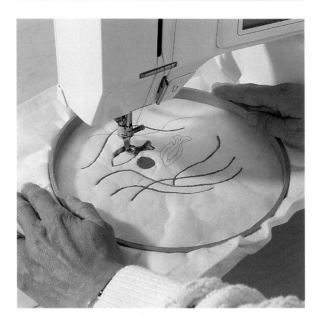

15. Moving the hoop in a side-to-side motion, fill the body of the fish with medium zigzag stitches.

16. Take a break and play—stitch the waves, repeating what you did in step 12.

17. For Fish #2, outline the body of the fish and its interior lines with 2 rows of small zigzag stitches. Remember to knot your stitches at the beginning and end of each line and clip only the upper thread.

18. With the stitch width at 0, outline the eye and then fill in the center of it with a small zig-zag stitch.

19. Change to a contrasting color and fill in the remaining unstitched areas of the fish. In small spaces, set the stitch width at 0.

You can continue to practice in any unused space, but stay away from the edge of the hoop.

troubleshooting

I hope you are having fun! If you are frustrated, chances are your machine needs further adjusting.

✦ If the top thread keeps breaking, the upper tension is too tight or the eye of the needle is too small. Check your needle first to make sure the thread has room to move. Some machine embroidery threads are 2- and 3-ply. Replace your needle after eight hours of use.

✦ If the upper thread is loopy, the upper tension is too loose, so tighten the upper tension.

✦ If the bobbin thread is showing on the top side, the top tension is too tight, and you need to loosen the top tension.

✦ If you are relaxed and sewing at a steady speed, the hoop will glide around much more smoothly, resulting in more even stitches.

✦ Remember, the faster you move the hoop, the longer the stitches will be.

> **TIP: Remember, to adjust the bobbin tension, turn right to tighten, left to loosen. Or, the lower the number, the looser the tension.**

machine embroidery

QUEEN TRIGGERFISH [42" x 39"]

Due to its tough skin, this fascinating fish is one of the few that can eat the spiny sea urchin. With a flip of its tail, it moves the urchin until the fleshy underside is exposed. The strange white-yellow-and-red creature is a sea cucumber. The red tentacles move like fingers to bring food to the cucumber's mouth.

Machine lace

Making machine lace is essentially stitching in open spaces. The two lace designs that I like to make are done inside an embroidery hoop. The size of the hoop you use determines the size of the shapes you can create. But the important thing to know is that the sky (or ocean, in this case) is the limit—play with shapes, stitching designs, and threads!

For this example, I used the coral shapes found in the "Andaman Island" tapestry (page 67, just to the left of the sponge), but feel free to draw your own shape.

There are a variety of stitching designs you can use. We'll practice two styles: linear and organic. The setup is the same for both. The direction of the stitches establishes the pattern in the design.

For the coral shapes in the "Andaman Island" tapestry, I made both Coral Pattern #1 and Coral Pattern #2 in the organic style.

materials

- ✦ Two 12" x 12" squares of fusible interfacing, such as Craft Bond, for each stitching pattern
- ✦ One 12" x 12" square of fleece for each technique
- ✦ 10" embroidery hoop
- ✦ Black polyester thread, for use on top and in the bobbin
- ✦ Size 100/16 sewing-machine needle (If this needle size is not available, use a 90/14 needle)
- ✦ Press cloth and iron

embroidery hoop setup

1. Cut two 12" squares of fusible interfacing and one 12" square of fleece for each piece of lace you plan to make.

2. Center the design and, with a pencil, trace a coral pattern (page 86) or draw a 3"-diameter circle onto the right side of one of the iron-on squares. Do not try to put more than one design in the hoop at the same time.

3. Using the press cloth, fuse the interfacing onto the fleece. Press the second square of interfacing onto the other side of the fleece.

4. Loosen the screw on the larger ring of your hoop. Lay it flat on a table and place the fabric, with the traced design facing up, over the hoop. Insert the smaller hoop ring on top and tighten the screw so that the fabric is taut.

5. Place the hoop under the needle.

machine setup

Use black thread on the top and in the bobbin.

1. Make sure the bobbin area of your machine is free of all lint.

2. Insert the needle and a darning or free-motion embroidery foot.

3. Adjust the upper and lower tension to reduce the tension. Remember, right to tighten and left to loosen. Adjust the bobbin screw at least $1/2$ turn. Reduce the upper tension by about two full numbers (from the "normal" setting). Test the stitch, using the space outside of the coral pattern.

4. Set the stitch width at 0.

5. Make sure that the feed dogs are *up*.

outline stitching

1. Lower the needle into the pencil line. Bring the bobbin thread to the top surface by holding the top thread taut and turning the handwheel.

2. Lower the presser foot and stitch a few stitches to knot the thread.

3. Using the pencil line as a guide, outline the coral with 3 rows of stitching, each row next to the previous one. Clip the threads.

4. Remove the embroidery foot and remove the hoop from the machine, *but do not take the fabric out of the hoop.* Using scissors or an X-acto™ knife, make a slit in the middle of the coral shape. Carefully cut away the inside area of the shape, cutting *up to the stitching.* Do not cut into the stitching.

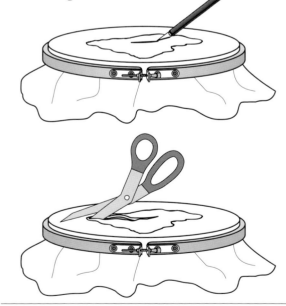

5. Lower the feed dogs and place the hoop under the needle. You have the option of stitching without a presser foot or inserting the darning or free-motion embroidery foot. The foot does add a bit of stability but it's difficult to see the bobbin thread as it forms stitches. I suggest you try this technique without a foot. If your top thread keeps breaking, insert the free-motion foot. Either way, *be sure to lower the presser bar*.

6. Lower the needle into the pencil line at the top edge of the coral and draw the bobbin thread to the top. Stitch a few stitches to knot the thread, holding the fabric down with your fingers close to the needle as you begin stitching. Be careful to keep your fingers from getting too close to the needle.

Now, imagine you are a spider about to weave your web!

linear design

1. With the stitch width set at 0 and a medium stitch length, stitch vertical lines straight across the open shape to the opposite side of the coral. Stitch a few anchoring stitches in the fabric, holding the fabric down with your fingers close to the needle. Do not cut the thread. Move over about 1/8" from the first line and stitch across the open space back to the top of the coral. Again, use your fingers to hold the fabric down each time the needle crosses the edge of the fabric and while you make anchoring stitches. Continue adding lines to fill the open space.

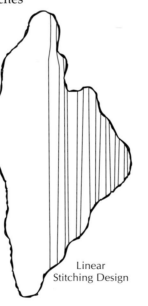

Linear Stitching Design

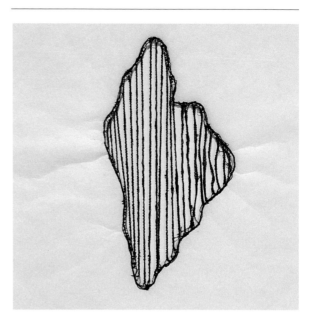

2. Next, join lines of stitching, two at a time. Set the zigzag stitch to a medium width. Center two lines of stitches under the needle. Stitch the two together, keeping the other lines of stitching out of the way. Again stitch to the opposite side of the shape. Anchor the stitching in the fabric as you did in step 1. Your line should be bumpy and wider. Use your fingers to carefully guide the two lines of stitching toward the needle. Try to keep one finger in front of the needle and one behind. Continue until all the stitched lines are joined in pairs. If you have an uneven number of stitched lines, you can join three threads or stitch another line.

3. Set the zigzag stitch to a narrow width. Starting at the top of the coral, stitch horizontal lines 1/8" to 1/4" apart across the open shape. Be sure to make anchoring stitches in the edge of the fabric, as you did in steps 1 and 2.

Now that you have established a grid, stitch across the open space, in any direction, making some lines wider by stitching over them a second time and joining others together. Use a medium stitch length.

machine lace

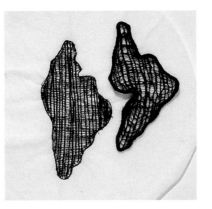

4. Remove the piece from the embroidery hoop and carefully cut away the fabric, *close to* the outline stitches. Using large zigzag stitches and the embroidery foot, stitch over any fabric, fleece, or interfacing that still shows around the outer edges. Keep the feed dogs down.

organic design

This technique is a little more challenging, but I love the results! Instead of stitching horizontal and vertical lines, you stitch diagonal lines.

1. Follow the steps in "Machine Setup" and "Outline Stitching" on pages 27–28.

2. Set the zigzag stitch width at 0. Make a few anchoring stitches in the fabric, holding the fabric down with your fingers close to the needle. Stitch diagonal lines across the open shape to the other side of the coral. Continue adding lines, stitching from one side of the open space to another until there is no more than 1/2" between lines.

Organic Stitching Design

3. Set the zigzag stitch width to medium. Randomly join the stitched lines into pairs or in groups of three. Skip from one line to the next, joining the lines as you sew. Vary the length of the stitching and the width of the zigzag stitch (from 0 to a medium width). Continue until you are pleased with the effect. If you feel that some of the spaces between the stitches are too open, set the zigzag to a 0 stitch width and add a few lines in the space. Then set the zigzag stitch to medium and join them randomly.

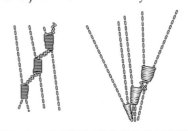

4. To finish, use the same technique as the linear design.

troubleshooting

A common problem with making lace is that the top thread often breaks. First, make sure the presser bar is down (even if there is no foot on the machine). Next, check the upper tension; if it is too tight, the thread will not pass through the tension disks easily, thereby breaking the thread.

Maintain an even, moderate speed. If you go too fast, the bobbin thread will get wrapped around the needle. If this happens, cut the threads and start again at the edge of the fabric.

TRUNKFISH [25" x 22"]

These boxy fish with bright circular patterns are dazzling. Multicolored corals surround the fish. Three gray-spotted trunkfish swim off in the background.

WHITE WAVES   [41" x 36¹/₂"]

While observing fish at the Houston Zoo, I saw a small yellow gopie, who was eating a bit of scallop, threatened by a beautiful angelfish. The gopie easily escaped into a hole he had dug in the sand. In the tapestry, black-and-white Crinoidea have attached themselves to turquoise corals, while a school of orange-tailed butterfly fish swim away.

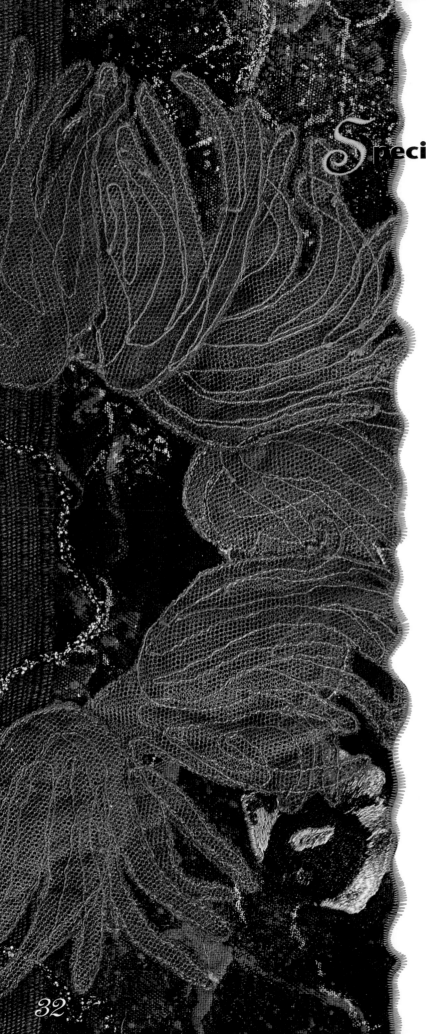

5pecial design effects with tulle

Some of the effects that I use are adapted from books or articles I have read. And, in the process of creating new art pieces, I have discovered other ways to achieve the effects that I wanted.

Variegated tulle opened a world of possibilities for me. I often use it to change the color of a fabric. The tulle's delicate color subtly alters the color of the fabric underneath it. I often use blue tulle over green fabric to give it a hue closer to that of the sea. Sometimes a fabric is too bright, and tulle tones it down, giving it a misty look. Like a veil, it provides a bit of mystery and intrigue. This is particularly effective in the "Andaman Island" tapestry on page 67.

In the "Rainbow Parrotfish" tapestry on page 37, I used layers of tulle over bits of fabric. Despite the variety of colors, the tulle united the fabrics, making the coral wall look three-dimensional.

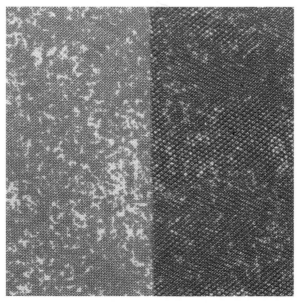

In the "Sea Anemones" tapestry on page 36, I used tulle to create a design shape.

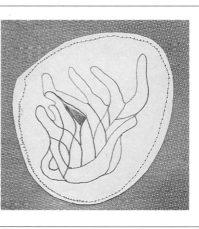

7. Pin or baste the drawing on top of the tulle.

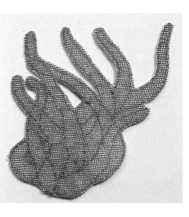

8. Using small straight stitches, stitch on all drawn lines of the design. Remove the paper. Cut away the excess tulle outside the stitching and within the shaded area indicated on the pattern. Be careful not to cut into the stitching.

techniques with tulle

Use the practice pattern on this page.

1. Use the same color embroidery thread on the top and in the bobbin.

2. Insert a size 60/8 needle, and your free-motion embroidery foot.

3. Reduce the upper tension (from the normal setting) by lowering it one number.

4. Trace the pattern onto paper, adding ½" all around the design as indicated by the dashed lines on the pattern.

5. Cut 2 squares of tulle ½" larger than your paper pattern.

6. Place 1 piece of tulle on top of the other. Set your iron on *low* and press the layered tulle to a piece of white or black interfacing, using a press cloth. The heat from the iron will fuse the tulle in place.

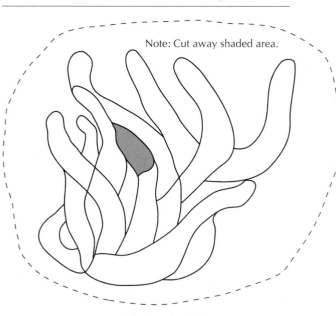

Note: Cut away shaded area.

Tulle Practice Pattern

coloring tulle

Sometimes I can't find the right color of variegated tulle to work with, so I purchase white tulle or netting and paint two layers of tulle at the same time. Tulle is so fine that often it takes two layers to be effective. I use water-based paint and fabric markers to color the tulle.

materials

Supplies for painting technique:

- ◆ Tulle or netting for 2 layers to cover the desired area
- ◆ 3 or more tubes of Liquitex® acrylic paint or other water-based paint that has the consistency of toothpaste (You want a paint that is thick enough to adhere to the netting. The samples are done in purple, turquoise, and blue paints.)
- ◆ Palette knife
- ◆ Large sponge
- ◆ Disposable tray or pan
- ◆ White poster board
- ◆ Plastic drop cloth
- ◆ Rubber gloves
- ◆ Paper towels

Supplies for fabric marker technique:

- ◆ Tulle or netting for 2 layers to cover the desired area
- ◆ 3 or more different colors of broad-tipped fabric markers (I used purple, blue, and green.)
- ◆ Plastic drop cloth

coloring tulle with paint

1. Lay poster board on a flat surface.

2. Cut 2 pieces of tulle the size that you need. Press out any wrinkles in the tulle with an iron set on *low.* Lay the 2 layers of tulle on top of each other and place them on the poster board.

3. With a palette knife, mix equal amounts of paint and water in your disposable tray.

4. Cut the sponge into smaller pieces. Dip a small sponge into the paint and brush it across the surface of the tulle, using arc or wavelike strokes. Excess paint will go through the holes in the tulle onto the poster board. Lift a corner of the tulle and use the sponge to wipe the excess paint off the poster board and reuse it.

5. Repeat step 4, alternating with the other colors to get the blended colors that you want. It's a good idea to practice blending colors until you find the combination that you want for your project.

6. Allow to dry for 24 hours, to set the paint.

coloring tulle with paint for a more muted effect

1. Cover your work area with a plastic drop cloth.

2. Dampen 2 layers of tulle with water. Squeeze out excess water. Place one layer of tulle over the other on the drop cloth. Press the tulle flat with your hands.

3. Mix and apply the paints to the tulle as you did in steps 4 and 5 on facing page. Colors will be more muted and will blend with each other.

4. Allow to dry for 24 hours.

TIP: If you notice that the paint has clogged up the mesh in the netting, unclog the hole with a sponge while the paint is still damp. If the paint has already dried, use a pin to push the paint out.

coloring tulle with fabric markers

1. Cover your work area with a plastic drop cloth.

2. Cut 2 pieces of tulle the size that you need. Press out any wrinkles in the tulle with an iron set on *low*. Lay the 2 layers of tulle on top of each other and place them on the drop cloth.

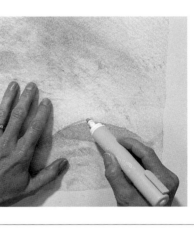

3. With a marker, "paint" the tulle using arc or wave-like strokes. To avoid streaks, go over the area 2 or 3 times to cover it evenly.

4. Repeat step 3, using the other colors.

5. Allow the paints to dry according to the directions on markers.

SEA ANEMONES [34" x 35"]

A symbiotic relationship exists between clown fish and poisonous anemones. While the anemones poison other fish, the clown fish swim freely among the tentacles. The variegated coney grouper in the center of the tapestry has been stung by the anemone, causing the coney grouper's colors to fade. Another grouper, in the lower right corner, has escaped. A variety of sponges and plants surrounds the fish. Three gray angelfish swim away. A tomato clown fish hides in the upper left corner.

RAINBOW PARROTFISH [39" x 31"]

A rainbow parrotfish emerges from a multicolored cave. The coral cave is composed of a variety of fabrics and layers of fine tulle. (The fused patchwork technique begins on page 44.) The school of wrasse swim freely in the blue-gray background.

$\mathcal{P}$ile stitching

I discovered this technique when I was trying to rip out rows of satin stitching that I was unhappy with. The end result is a fuzzy texture. Like wild grass, it "blows" in all directions. It works well when combined with straight stitching. The two complement each other, and the pile appears thicker and taller when placed next to the straight embroidery. I used this technique to create blue and purple vegetation in the "Sea Anemones" tapestry on page 36. It makes the plants appear as though they are swaying with the current of the water, and the fish look like they are hiding. Use this technique where you want a fluffy or downy texture.

1. Cut 6" squares from fabric, paper-backed fusible web, and tear-away stabilizer.

2. Press the fusible web to the wrong side of the fabric. Remove the paper backing. Place the fabric piece on top of the stabilizer and baste them together.

3. Insert an embroidery foot on your machine. Be sure to use a foot that has a groove cut out on the underside of the foot.

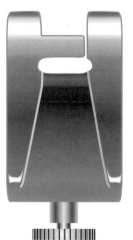

(Enlarged to show detail)

4. Insert a size 75/11 or 80/12 embroidery needle.

5. Set the zigzag to the widest stitch possible.

6. Set the stitch length at the shortest length, but make sure the fabric still feeds properly through the needle.

7. Reduce the top tension by one number from the normal setting.

8. Thread the top of the machine with embroidery thread. Variegated thread works well with this technique. Use basting thread in the bobbin.

9. Make a row of satin stitching.

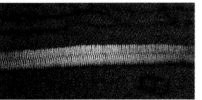

10. Stitch another row next to it, just catching the edge of the first row.

11. Place a sharp seam ripper under the first row of stitching and cut through the center of the satin stitching. Be careful not to cut into the fabric.

12. Push the cut threads toward the middle of the two stitched rows. Stitch on each side of the middle, with the stitch width and length at the same settings. Do not stitch over the cut threads that you pushed toward the middle.

13. Cut the rows of stitching that you just made, as you did in step 11.

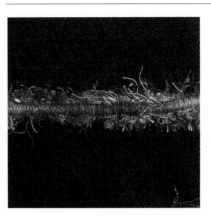

14. Push the threads toward the middle of the stitched rows. Stitch again, this time stitching over the cut threads. You will not be able to catch all the threads with one row. Continue adding rows of stitches and cutting them until you have the width and thickness you want. The layers of thread will create a full, thick line.

15. Set the stitch width at 0 and replace the foot with a free-motion embroidery foot.

16. Lower the needle into the fabric. Bring the bobbin thread to the top surface. Lower the presser foot and stitch a few stitches to knot the thread. Clip the thread tails. Stitch freely, as if drawing. Do stitch over the cut threads to prevent them from pulling out. Stitch over just once or twice, because you do not want to flatten all of your work.

FILEFISH [27" x 19"]

Three small damselfish watch as the scrawled filefish grazes on plant life. The filefish has a tiny mouth; consequently, it takes longer to feed than most fish.

NIGHT VISIONS [29" x 33"]

Clown fish and black damselfish swim together in the dark waters. A small four-eye butterfly fish investigates a small colony of anemones. In the foreground, a barred hamlet moves cautiously toward the anemones. Variegated metallic thread is stitched on top of the background fabric to create wavelike movement in the water. The seaweed on the right adds dimension and unites the double border. (The twisted-and-textured-cords technique for the seaweed begins on page 42.)

Twisted and textured cords

I have used variations of this technique for years. The basic premise is to use strips of fabric, cord, or yarn and twist them together. I make seaweed for my tapestries using these techniques. In the "Night Visions" tapestry on page 41, I frayed the edges of fabric strips, stitched tulle or sheer fabrics down the center, then, with the sheer fabric to the outside, twisted the strips. Twisted cords would also make interesting tree trunks, branches, vines, wires, and even umbilical cords. They add extra dimension to your tapestries.

1. Select 2 different colors or values (light and dark) of fabric to create contrast. In each fabric, clip the selvage and pull a thread to find the true grain of the fabric. Cut or tear the fabric along the edge where the thread was removed. This establishes a straight line for the fringed edge.

2. Cut a 1¹/₄" x 14" strip from each fabric.

3. Fringe the edges of the fabric strips ¹/₄" on each side by pulling lengthwise threads from the edge.

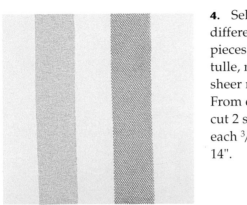

4. Select 2 different pieces of tulle, net, or sheer nylon. From each, cut 2 strips, each $3/4$" x 14".

5. Center a tulle strip on top of each fabric strip. Use invisible nylon or matching thread to stitch down the centers of the strips.

6. Place the strips wrong sides together and stitch down the center to make one reversible strip.

7. Select a background fabric.

8. Pin one end of the strip to the background fabric to anchor it, then stitch it in place by machine, close to the end of the strip.

9. Twist the strip, then pin the unanchored end in place. Machine stitch it to the background.

To make a single-color, wider cord

A simpler variation is to fringe one strip of fabric without the added tulle and without making it reversible. Twist and sew a strip of fabric as in steps 8–9.

1. Fringe a strip of fabric in the width that you desire.

2. Twist the strip.

3. Bring the 2 ends together, folding the strip in half.

4. Twist again to make the strip tighter.

5. Pin the ends together and stitch.

Fused patchwork

This technique is a lot of fun! You can produce a variety of effects, depending on your choices of fabrics and threads, the number of layers you have, and the sheer fabrics that you add to the top. I created the background of the "Rainbow Parrotfish" on page 37, using several layers of fabric and a layer of tulle.

materials

- ✦ Assorted fabric scraps for practice (4" x 4" squares work well)
- ✦ 12" x 12" square of paper-backed fusible web, such as Wonder-Under or Aleene's Fusible Web™
- ✦ 12" x 12" square of medium-weight fusible interfacing, such as Craft Bond by Pellon
- ✦ 12" x 12" square of background fabric*
- ✦ 12" x 12" square of tulle
- ✦ Invisible nylon thread, such as Wonder or Stitch Thru
- ✦ Basting thread, such as Brooks basting thread by J. & P. Coats, or a cotton embroidery thread
- ✦ Size 75/11 or 80/12 machine-embroidery needle
- ✦ Free-motion embroidery foot

Small areas of this will show. In my tapestry, I used a hand-dyed blue fabric. Use a fabric that blends with your other fabrics.

directions

1. Fuse the craft fusible web to the wrong side of your 4" squares of fabrics. Do not remove the paper backing if you prefer to draw shapes before you cut them. If you prefer to cut your shapes freehand, remove the paper.

2. Cut shapes out of your fabrics.

3. Press the fusible interfacing to the wrong side of the background fabric.

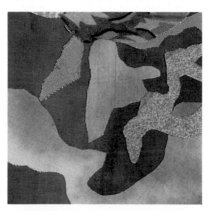

4. Arrange a layer of fabric shapes on the background fabric. Fuse them in place. Let them cool, then add another layer of shapes, overlapping them to get the desired effect.

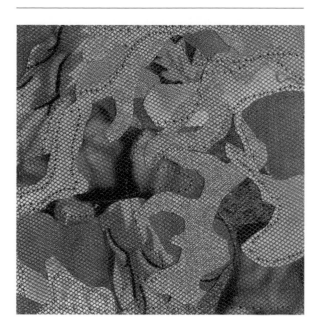

8. Machine quilt through all layers. Quilt in a pattern that you like or outline the fused shapes, stitching about $\frac{1}{8}$" inside the edges.

5. Lay tulle over the entire piece and baste in place.

6. Thread the top of the machine with the invisible nylon thread. Use basting thread in the bobbin.

7. Insert a new size 75/11 or 80/12 embroidery needle. Reduce the top tension by one number from the normal setting. Test the stitching on a scrap of fabric.

Satin-stitch edging for appliqué

Appliqué allows me to bring a variety of shapes and color into my work. The embroidered fish is my detailed design element. The background provides the foundation and is reminiscent of water. Appliqué is the design bridge between the embroidered fish and the waterlike background. Plants, coral, and schools of fish are appliquéd, depicting the environment.

To create depth in the coral in the "Clown Triggerfish" tapestry on page 49, I layered different colors on top of each other. Varying the colors of thread and the width of the stitches made it come alive with movement.

In the tapestry "Harlequin Tuskfish" on page 15, I appliquéd orange and cream-colored silk fabrics together, joining them with blue variegated thread. Although the color of the thread is so dominant, it looks as if it belongs on the fish; it doesn't look like an appliqué technique.

materials

- ◆ ¹/₂ yd. fabric for background
- ◆ Assorted fabric scraps for appliqué pieces (5" x 7" pieces are ideal)
- ◆ ¹/₂ yd. paper-backed fusible web, such as HeatnBond
- ◆ ¹/₂ yd. tear-away stabilizer, such as Stitch-n-Tear by Pellon
- ◆ Embroidery thread in assorted colors that contrast and blend with the appliqué fabrics
- ◆ Basting thread
- ◆ Size 75/11 machine-embroidery needle
- ◆ Iron and press cloth

machine setup

1. Insert a new size 75/11 embroidery needle.

2. Reduce the top tension by one number from the normal setting so that only the top thread shows on the front side of the tapestry. Some of the top thread will show on the wrong side of the tapestry.

3. Thread the top of the machine with embroidery thread. Use basting thread in the bobbin.

4. Insert a free-motion embroidery foot.

5. Make sure the feed dogs are *up*.

Appliqué pattern (reversed)

Trace this onto paper side of fusible web.

appliqué practice

1. Cut 4" x 6½" rectangles from a piece of appliqué fabric and from fusible web.

2. Trace the appliqué pattern (reversed) on page 46 onto the paper side of the fusible web. Cut out the shape on the traced line.

3. Center the fusible-web shape on the wrong side of the fabric rectangle. Fuse it in place.

4. Following the shape of the fusible web, cut out the appliqué piece.

5. Remove the paper backing from the fusible web. Fuse the appliqué piece to the right side of the background fabric.

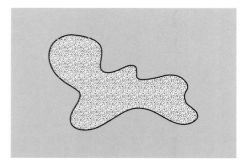

6. From the tear-away stabilizer, cut a piece the same size as the background fabric.

7. Baste or pin the stabilizer to the fabric. Now let's sew!

TIP: Set the stitch width at 0 when you begin and end zigzag stitching to lock, or knot, the stitches.

design ideas to try

Depending on the effects you want to achieve, there are a number of ways to vary stitch widths and thread colors. Try these, then develop your own combinations.

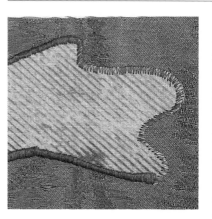

◆ When satin-stitching the edges of appliqué pieces, be sure to completely cover the edges to prevent the fabric from fraying. Use zigzag stitches that are wide enough to cover the edges. I tend to set a small stitch length to create a strong line. Play with different stitch widths and lengths to discover the ones that you like best. By moving the fabric quickly, stitches will be farther apart, while moving slowly creates tighter stitches.

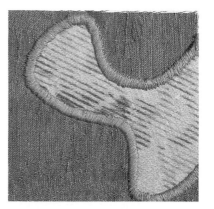

◆ The thread colors you choose for the top make a big difference. If you want the appliqué to blend, choose a thread that matches the background fabric or one that blends with it.

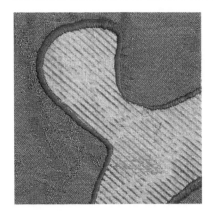

✦ Practice changing the stitch width as you sew along the edge, varying it from wide to narrow. Be sure the needle is in the *up* position when you change the stitch width, to keep from breaking the needle or damaging your machine.

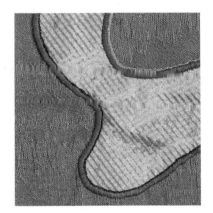

✦ Another satin-stitch effect that I like is outlining around the first row of stitching in a contrasting color. After you have finished satin-stitching the edge of the appliqué, change the top thread color. Set the zigzag stitch width to a narrow width. Stitch inside or outside the satin-stitched edge. Move in a side-to-side motion. This creates an outline. On the inside, I used a hot-pink thread to create contrast, while on the outside edge, I used a color similar to the background to create a blending effect. This technique is great for creating dimension.

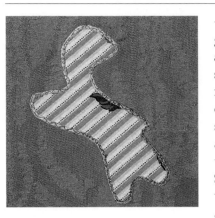

✦ Another great effect is achieved by stitching a narrow stitch over a wide satin stitch in a contrasting thread color. Set the stitch width at 0 and pretend you are drawing with your needle and thread! Relax and play! This is often how I discover what I like and what I can incorporate into my work.

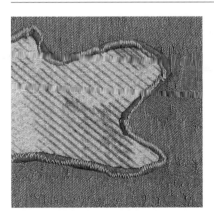

✦ If you don't have a thread color that you want, select a color that blends with the background fabric and one that blends with the appliqué piece. Stitch around the appliqué piece with a wide stitch width in a bright color. Then with a duller color, stitch over the bright-colored stitching. Vary the width of the stitch randomly.

There are so many possibilities. Try different threads, especially variegated colors. Refer to pages 16–17 for more ideas on threads. Play with different combinations of stitch widths to create different effects.

CLOWN TRIGGERFISH [21" x 30"]

A distinctive clown triggerfish swims away from coral masses. Below, bright pink damselfish glide

through the water. A thin-striped velvet background is heavily quilted to give the illusion of movement.

ndaman island tapestry

This tapestry is a great way for you to practice the techniques that I have presented in this book. I also introduce a new technique—unweaving—to make the three-dimensional sponge.

I encourage you to study the color photograph of the tapestry on page 67 and substitute your own color choices. Enjoy your "swim" under the sea!

materials and supplies

The materials list includes everything you need to complete the tapestry.

fabrics

54"–60"-wide decorator fabric

✦ 1 yd. blue textured fabric for background

✦ 1 yd. blue fabric (medium weight) for backing

✦ Assorted fabric scraps for appliqué pieces

> 12" x 12" dark blue print for Template 1
>
> 10" x 11" medium blue print for Template 2
>
> 9" x 14" purple and beige print sheer fabric for Template 3
>
> 10" x 10" purple print for Templates 4 and 5
>
> 8" x 9" orange and blue print for Template 6
>
> 9" x 10" light blue print for Template 7
>
> 10" x 14" black, pink, and green print for Templates 8, 11, 17, and 20
>
> 10" x 18" black and green print for Templates 9, 12, 13, 18, 19, 21, and 22
>
> 10" x 14" purple and green print for Templates 10, 14, and 16
>
> 3" x 3" light green print for Template 15
>
> 10" x 18" black, gold, and blue print for Template 23
>
> 11" x 27" black and gold print for Template 24

✦ ¼ yd. black cotton velvet for border

✦ 1 yd. blue tulle

✦ ⅓ yd. iridescent silk for the sponge*

✦ 2 yds. paper-backed fusible web, such as Wonder-Under, HeatnBond, or Aleene's

✦ 2 yds. tear-away stabilizer

✦ 1 yd. fleece, such as Thermolam

Sometimes, iridescent silk can be difficult to find. Loosely woven fabrics in a natural fiber such as cotton and wool work well, too. As alternatives, hand weave or crochet the sponge pattern pieces. The effect that you want is textured and nubby.

threads

- A variety of machine-embroidery thread to complement the appliqué fabrics
- Black, white, yellow, orange, and variegated yellow machine-embroidery thread for the fish
- 1 large spool of black polyester thread for the lace coral
- Invisible nylon thread for machine quilting
- Cotton basting thread in a color that blends with the backing fabric, such as Brooks basting thread by J. & P. Coats, or 50-weight cotton sewing thread
- Blue, black, and pink standard sewing thread

tools

- 10" embroidery hoop
- Small, sharp embroidery scissors
- One package of machine-embroidery needles, size 75/11 or 80/12
- Size 90/14 machine-embroidery or topstitching needles, for stitching the embroidered fish onto the background
- Needle-nose tweezers (the type used for sergers)
- Rotary cutter, cutting mat, and rulers
- Nickel-plated safety pins
- 4 bicycle clips
- Free-motion embroidery foot
- Even-feed (walking) foot

machine appliqué

Create the undersea boulders and valleys by machine appliquéing the background pieces in place.

machine setup

1. Insert a new size 75/11 embroidery needle.

2. Reduce the top tension by one number from the normal setting so that only the top thread shows on the front side of the tapestry. Some of the top thread will show on the wrong side of the tapestry.

3. Insert a free-motion embroidery foot.

4. Thread the top of the machine with embroidery thread. Use basting thread in the bobbin.

5. Review "Satin-Stitch Edging for Appliqué," beginning on page 46.

satin-stitching and appliqué

Refer to the Fabrics list on page 50 when cutting the appliqué pieces. Andaman Island appliqué patterns are on the pullout pattern.

1. From the background fabric, cut a 26" x 31" rectangle. Press.

2. Align the lower left corner of the background fabric with the lower left corner of the pattern. The 26"-long side of the rectangle runs the width of the tapestry. With a pencil, trace the design lines from the pattern onto the right side of the fabric, beginning with appliqué piece 24.

3. From the tear-away stabilizer, cut a piece the same size as the background rectangle. Place it on the wrong side of background fabric. Baste the 2 layers together around the outside edges.

4. Beginning with appliqué piece 1, trace each pattern piece on tracing paper. Flip paper over.

The appliqué pieces are stitched to the background in numerical order, beginning with piece 1. The appliqué pieces that lie underneath other pieces must have seam allowances added to some of the edges. Refer to the Seam Allowance Guides on pages 89–90 to add $1/2$"-wide seam allowances to *some* of the edges of the appliqué pieces. Note that seam allowances are added to edges of pieces that are adjacent to pieces with a higher number. For instance, piece 14 is adjacent to pieces 19 and 23, which both have higher numbers. Referring to the Seam Allowance Guide, you see that $\frac{1}{2}$"-wide seam allowances must be added to the left and right edges of piece 14.

The dashed line that is marked $\frac{1}{2}$" inside the perimeter of the pattern indicates the seam allowance for the outside edges of the tapestry.

5. Fuse the web to the wrong side of the appliqué fabric. Cut out the piece on the pencil line. Remove the backing paper.

6. Fuse piece 1 in place to background fabric.

7. Using thread in a compatible color, satin-stitch the edges of the piece that will not be covered by another appliqué piece.

8. Repeat steps 4–7 for appliqué pieces 2–15.

9. Trace appliqué piece 16 onto the paper side of a piece of fusible web. Trim around the shape, adding about $\frac{1}{4}$" all around. Fuse the web to the wrong side of the appliqué fabric. Cut out the piece on the pencil line. Remove backing paper.

10. Fuse the piece in place onto the wrong side of another piece of the same fabric, to make the piece reversible. This is the sponge pocket.

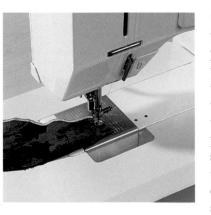

11. Using the sponge pocket pattern, mark the stitching triangles onto the appliqué piece. Satin-stitch along the upper edge of the sponge pocket, between the two triangles.

12. Pin the pocket in place on the background fabric. Machine baste the pocket in place, along the lower edge, where there are no satin stitches.

13. Repeat steps 4–7 for appliqué pieces 17–24.

14. Trim away excess threads. Do not remove the tear-away stabilizer from the back of the background fabric until the fish are sewn in place.

machine embroidering the fish

The fish are created inside an embroidery hoop. After all the fish are stitched, they are trimmed around the outside edge, leaving just enough fabric to baste the fish onto the fabric background. The final stitching around the edges is done when the fish are attached to the background fabric.

machine setup

1. Insert a 75/11 or 80/12 embroidery needle.

2. Insert a darning or free-motion embroidery foot.

3. Thread the top of the machine with black embroidery thread. Use basting thread (white or black) in the bobbin.

4. Lower the feed dogs.

stitching the black-and-white striped fish

The fish patterns are on pages 82–83. Trace them exactly as they are oriented on the pattern sheet. The patterns indicate which areas to stitch in black (B), white (W), and yellow (Y).

1. Cut a 12" x 12" piece of fusible interfacing (2" larger than your hoop). Using the fish patterns, position the pattern under the piece of interfacing, so that Fish #5 is in the center. Trace the designs onto the interfacing, noting the stitching-direction arrows and thread colors.

2. Cut a piece of fleece the same size as the interfacing. Fuse the interfacing to the fleece.

3. Cut a piece of tear-away stabilizer the same size as the fleece. Place the stabilizer on the other side of the fleece. Baste the 3 layers together all around the outside edge to make a "sandwich."

4. Place the sandwich in the embroidery hoop, as described in "Tips to Avoid Pitfalls" on this page. Now you are ready to stitch!

5. Place your hoop on top of the throat plate of your machine.

TIPS TO AVOID PITFALLS

✦ Make a habit of lowering the presser bar before you begin stitching.

✦ Each time you begin and end stitching, knot the threads by making a few stitches with the stitch length set at 0, then trim the top tail thread.

✦ Refer to "Embroidery Hoop Setup" on pages 20–21. Place the traced fish design *face up* (interfacing side of the "sandwich") on top of the outer (larger) ring. Insert the smaller ring inside. Push the smaller hoop ring down inside the outer ring so that it extends beyond the outer ring to create a $1/8$" lip. Tighten the screw. Trim excess fabric to within 1" of the outer edge of the hoop.

✦ The fish patterns show the direction of the stitches. It is important to be consistent so that all the fish will look the same.

✦ If your fabric buckles while you are stitching, remove the hoop from the machine. Take the "sandwich" out of the hoop; use a press cloth to gently press it with a dry iron set on *cotton*. Clip the bobbin threads. Place the piece back in the hoop and start again. Some buckling will occur between the fish because of the contrast between areas that contain concentrated stitches and areas that do not have stitching.

✦ Replace your needle after 8 hours of sewing. This will save you a lot of frustration.

✦ Relax! Think of this as painting and sing "Here we go loop to loop!"

6. Starting with Fish #3 and black embroidery thread, lower the needle into the center of a black area. Draw the bobbin thread to the top. Stitch a few stitches in place to knot the thread.

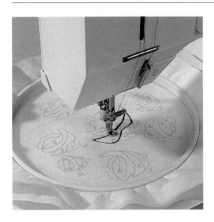

7. Stitch over to the edge of the black section, using a medium-length straight stitch. Using narrow zig-zag stitches, outline the black area. Be careful to stitch up to, but not across, the outside edge of the fish. Do not worry if you occasionally stitch into an adjacent area of the fish, because it will be covered by stitches when you get to that section.

8. Fill the area within the outline stitches with medium zig-zag stitches, stitching in the directions indicated on the patterns. Knot the thread by changing the stitch width back to 0 and move to the next black area. Repeat step 6. The eye areas are black and can be done by outlining the areas with straight stitches, then filling in with narrow zigzag stitches. Continue until the black sections of all the fish in your hoop are completed. Trim away excess threads on the front and back of the work.

9. Stitch the white sections of the fish, repeating the same steps as for the black areas. Each fish has 3 white sections: the area closest to the caudal (rear) fin, the stripe that has the long dorsal fin, and the face. I have included just a hint of the dorsal fin on the fish patterns. More fin will be stitched directly onto the background fabric. A basic guideline is, if an area is 1/8" or narrower and adjacent to the outside edge, stitch it after it is basted onto the background. Again, trim away excess threads.

10. Although the yellow fins are quite small, it is helpful to stitch them anyway. It defines the area, adds color, and makes it easier when applying them to the background fabric. (The more detail you embroider now, the less you will have to do later when the fish are stitched to the background and there are more layers to sew through.) Stitch the yellow areas with narrow zigzag stitches. You now have half of the fish ready to jump into the water!

11. Remove the sandwich from the hoop. Cut out each fish along the outside edges, leaving about a 1/16"-wide lip all around so they can be stitched to the background fabric.

12. Starting with step 1, repeat the same process for the fish patterns on page 83. Center Fish #1 in the center of the interfacing. Notice that the fin on the right side of Fish #1 is stitched in yellow.

13. The tear-away stabilizer should still be on the back of your tapestry. Make sure it has not pulled away from the area where the fish will be sewn. If it has puckered or torn, replace it with a new piece.

14. Referring to the Black-and-White Striped Fish Placement Guide on the pullout pattern insert, hand baste the fish in place on your tapestry with white basting thread. Make sure you catch the tear-away stabilizer while you baste. Fish #4, #5, #6, and #9 lie on top of other fish, so set them aside until the fish under them are completed. Be sure to use a thimble while you baste! This step takes time, so be patient!

15. Insert a new size 90/14 needle and your free-motion embroidery foot. Lower the feed dogs.

16. Starting with Fish #7 and yellow embroidery thread, stitch the fin areas first. Draw the bobbin thread to the top and knot with a few stitches. Use a straight stitch

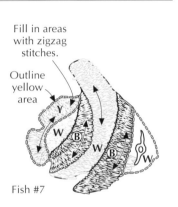

Fill in areas with zigzag stitches.

Outline yellow area

Fish #7

to outline the area, fill in with small- to medium-width zigzag stitches. Follow the stitching directions as you did before so that the rows of stitching blend into each other.

17. Stitch the fin areas of all of the fish. Trim away excess threads on the front and back of your work.

18. Stitch the black areas of all of the fish. Again, trim away excess threads.

19. Referring to the Black-and-White Striped Fish Placement Guide on the pullout pattern, use white chalk to draw the top (dorsal) fin of each fish except for Fish #3, #5, #6, and #9, onto the background fabric. Each fin is approxi-

mately 1½" long, and its widest point is at the top of the head. It tapers to a single straight stitch at the tip.

20. With white thread, begin with a straight stitch near the head and follow along the chalk line to the tip. At the tip, keep the needle in the fabric, pivot the fabric, and stitch back toward the head. This outlines both sides of the fin. With medium-width zigzag stitches, stitch just inside the outline, up to ¼" from the tip of the fin. Continue filling in the fin area. For Fish #3, just cover the sides and edge of the top fin with small zigzag stitches.

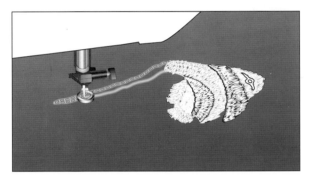

21. For the other white areas, use small zigzag stitches. Now you can remove any remaining pins and remove the stabilizer. Yippee! You are almost finished with your school of Black-and-White Striped Fish (*Heniochus acuminatus*). The next step will be a new and exciting challenge.

22. Complete the embroidery of Fish #4, outside the hoop. Beginning in the lower black fin, carefully stitch with medium-width zigzag stitches over the edge of the fin. Cover any fabric that may still show, using the correct thread colors. Baste Fish #4 in place on the background. Notice that the bottom fin of Fish #4 abuts the top fin of Fish #3. Finish stitching the other areas of the fish as you did in steps 20 and 21, except, this time you do not have a top fin to stitch.

23. Finish Fish #5, which is still not stitched to the background fabric. Since most of it will cover Fish #4, you will do all the stitching (except for the top fin) directly on the machine. Start with yellow and stitch over the fins. A medium stitch length works best; it bites into the previous stitches and covers the edge. Do not worry if it looks a bit bumpy. Knot and change to black thread. Using the same technique, finish the top and bottom black stripes. Trim your threads and switch to white thread. Stitch the face and the bottom white stripe.

24. Pin Fish #5 in place. Using a narrow zigzag stitch, tack the face down at the edge, about where the nose or mouth would be. Do not attempt to do a row of stitching. You are making a bar tack. Make another bar tack in the middle of the bottom white stripe. Remove the pin. Draw the top fin with chalk and stitch.

25. Adding Fish #9 to the tapestry is a little different because its top fin covers the tail fin of Fish #8. First complete the embroidery of Fish #9, outside the hoop. Beginning with black

thread, freely stitch the top edge of the 2 narrow black stripes. With yellow thread, freely stitch the edge of the tail fin. Finish with white thread, stitching the edge of the face and over the edges of the top fin. It will look a bit bumpy, but that is normal.

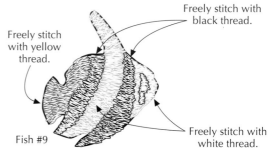

Freely stitch with black thread.

Freely stitch with yellow thread.

Freely stitch with white thread.

Fish #9

26. Pin or baste Fish #9 in place. Using the Black-and-White Striped Fish Placement Guide, draw the top fin on the background with chalk. Stitch the fish to the background with a few bar tacks. Then, follow the drawn line to complete the embroidery of the fish as you did for the Black-and-White Striped Fish in step 20, page 55.

27. To complete the embroidery of Fish #6, finish stitching the white edges where it will overlap Fish #3. Then, baste it in place onto the background. Draw the top fin on the background with chalk, referring to the Black-and-White Striped Fish Placement Guide. Tack the fish in place as you did before, then follow the drawn line to complete the embroidery. Stitch the remaining edges of Fish #6 (that do not overlap Fish #3) to the background with medium-width zigzag stitches.

Congratulations! You have completed a beautiful school of Black-and-White Striped Fish!

stitching the yellowhead wrasse fish

The patterns are on page 84. Trace them exactly as they are oriented on the page. The fish are stitched in black, orange, and variegated yellow embroidery thread.

1. Cut a 12" x 12" piece of fusible interfacing (2" larger than your hoop). Position the pattern under the piece of interfacing so that Fish #3 is in the center. Trace the designs onto the interfacing, noting the stitching-direction arrows.

2. Cut a piece of fleece the same size as the interfacing. Fuse the interfacing to the fleece.

3. Cut a piece of tear-away stabilizer the same size as the fleece. Place the stabilizer on the other side of the fleece. Baste the 3 layers together all around the outside edge to make a "sandwich."

4. Place the sandwich in the hoop, as described in "Tips to Avoid Pitfalls," on page 53.

5. Place your hoop on top of the throat plate of your machine.

6. Starting with Fish #3 and black embroidery thread, stitch the eyes and black spot on the top fin of each fish. Remember to draw the bobbin thread to the top and to stitch a few stitches in place to knot the thread when you begin and before you move to the next black area. Use narrow zigzag stitches to fill in the areas. Continue until the black sections of all the fish are completed. Trim away excess threads on the front and back of your work.

7. Repeating the same steps as for the black areas, stitch the orange areas of the fish. These areas include the oval shapes around the black eyes and the oval shapes behind the eyes. Trim away excess threads.

8. Stitch the remaining areas of the fish with variegated yellow thread. Using narrow zigzag stitches, stitch all around the outside edges of the fish. Fill the open areas within the outline stitches with medium zigzag stitches. Stitch in the directions indicated on the patterns. Complete all 4 fish in the same manner.

9. Remove the sandwich from the hoop. Carefully cut out each fish, as close to the embroidered edges as possible without cutting into the stitching.

10. Complete the embroidery of each fish outside the hoop. Using the variegated yellow thread, stitch around the outside edges of each fish, with medium zigzag stitches. You're now ready to put the Yellowhead Wrasse Fish in the water! Set Fish #4 aside until the sponge is in place.

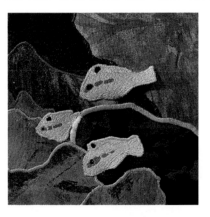

11. Referring to the Yellowhead Wrasse Fish Placement Guide on the pullout pattern, pin each fish in place. Note that the tail of Fish #1 is under sponge pocket (appliqué piece 16), and the head is on top of appliqué piece 13. Fish #2's head is on top of appliqué pieces 8 and 9, and its tail will be covered by the coral. The head of Fish #3 is on top of appliqué piece 19, and the tail will be covered by the coral.

12. Stitch the fish to the background with a few bar tacks. Fish #3 is bartacked at the head only.

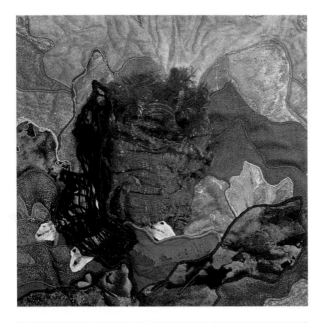

2. Starting with the sponge cuff, pull the horizontal threads from the top edge (side A) to make a 1"-wide fringed edge.

making the sponge

This is a really fun way to create a piece that has the look of a handwoven textile. It is similar to pulled-thread embroidery and almost looks "unwoven."

The sponge and sponge cuff patterns are on pages 85–86.

3. With the tweezers, gently loosen the next 1/2" of the fringed edge. Push the threads randomly from the unfringed area into the frayed area to create a wavelike pattern. Repeat until you are pleased with the effect.

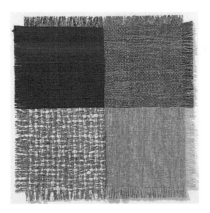

1. From the silk, cut out the sponge and sponge cuff.

4. Starting at least 3" from the fringed edge of side A, use tweezers to pull 3 horizontal threads in random places, to form loops. Then, pull up 3 or more threads and cut them. About 1 1/2" away from the cut threads, pull the same threads up with your tweezers, forming loops about 1/4" high. The cut threads will be pulled back into the fabric when you pull up the loops.

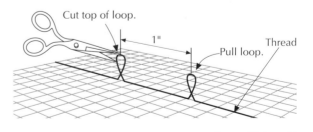

Cut top of loop.

1"

Thread

Pull loop.

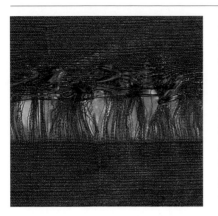

5. Pull a few more horizontal threads and remove them, creating an open space. Using tweezers, manipulate the threads into the open area by pushing and pulling the threads randomly in different directions.

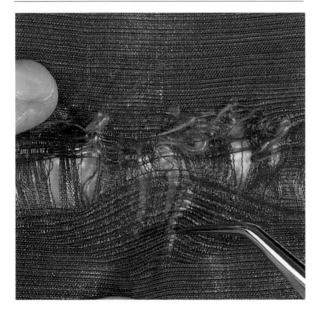

6. Continue pulling, cutting, and manipulating, repeating steps 4 and 5. Stop 1" inside the edge of side B.

7. With right sides together, fold the cuff in half, matching the two short sides (sides C). Using a $1/2$"-wide seam allowance, sew the edges together. Set aside.

8. On the sponge, pull the horizontal threads from the edge of side A in the same manner as you did in step 2 for the sponge cuff, to make a $1/2$"-wide fringed edge.

9. Create loops, using the technique in step 4, spacing them randomly about $1^1/_2$" apart.

10. Continue, following steps 3–6, until the sponge piece looks textured with pulls and loops, like a contemporary weaving. Stop 1" inside the edge of Side B.

11. On the right-hand side of the sponge, 2" down from the top fringed edge and 1" inside the right edge, mark a gathering line. Stitch a line of long gathering stitches on this line as shown. Do not gather the stitches yet.

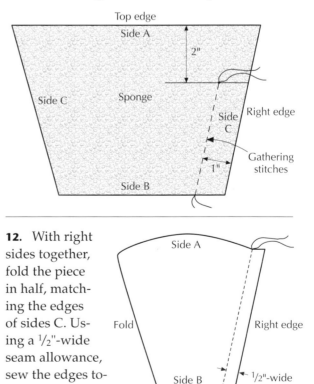

12. With right sides together, fold the piece in half, matching the edges of sides C. Using a $1/2$"-wide seam allowance, sew the edges together.

13. Pull the gathering thread until the fabric is about 1½" shorter. Hand-stitch over the gathers to create small tucks.

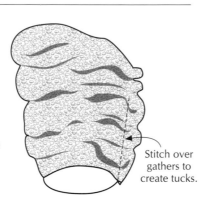

Stitch over gathers to create tucks.

14. Place the cuff inside the sponge, tucking the unfringed edge (side B) inside. Matching the seams, pin the cuff and sponge together. Stitch them together by hand, ½" from the bottom edge of the cuff.

15. Place the sponge inside the sponge pocket (appliqué piece 17). Place the seams to the back so that they do not show. Play with the piece until you are pleased with how it looks. Pin in place. Stitch by machine or by hand to the background, stitching under the gathers and inside the cuff where they will not be visible from the right side.

16. Place Fish #4 partially behind the sponge pocket (appliqué piece 16) with its head tucked into the sponge. Pin, then bartack the fish in place.

making the lace coral

1. Refer to "Machine Lace" on pages 26–29. Use Coral patterns #1 and #2 on page 86 to make one of each. Stitch them both with black thread, using the organic design described on page 29.

2. Using the Appliqué Placement Guide, pin Coral #1 in place.

3. With the same black thread and a free-motion embroidery foot, stitch the coral to the background in the places indicated on the bottom edges of appliqué pieces 16 and 20 and on the top edge of appliqué piece 7.

4. Pin the top of Coral #2 to appliqué piece 7 in the place indicated on the template. Stitch in place.

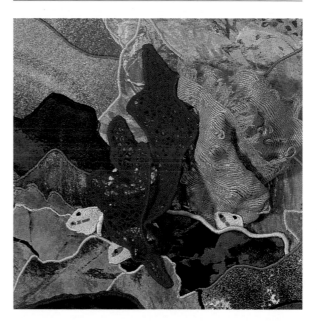

5. Twist the coral to the left one turn, then pin it next to Coral #1. Stitch in place.

machine quilting

Machine quilting is a challenge if your work surface isn't flat and big enough to accommodate the size of the tapestry. Having a work-surface level with the throat plate of your machine allows the weight of your tapestry to be evenly distributed.

If your space doesn't allow for more table area, it is helpful to roll your piece so that the weight of it doesn't prevent you from moving it easily while you are quilting. Bicycle clips work well for keeping your piece rolled. As you quilt, reroll the piece.

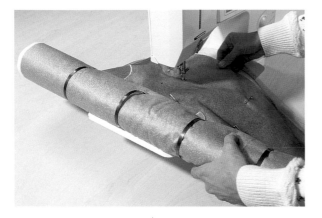

After all the appliqué and machine-embroidered elements are completed, the tapestry is ready to be quilted.

I prefer to add the border after the tapestry is machine quilted because often the tapestry "shrinks" or becomes distorted during machine quilting. "Square up" the outside edges of the tapestry after the quilting is completed.

1. Measure your tapestry through the center in both directions. Cut a piece of fleece to those measurements, plus twice the width of your border. For example, if your tapestry is 25" x 29" and the finished border width is 1$\frac{1}{2}$" wide, cut a piece of fleece 28" x 32".

2. Press your backing fabric, then cut a piece the same size as the fleece.

3. Lay the backing wrong side up on a flat surface. Smooth out any wrinkles. Lay the fleece on top of the backing.

4. Lay the tapestry on top of the batting, centering it. Smooth out any wrinkles.

5. Starting in the center, pin through all layers with safety pins. Do not pin through the sponge, sponge pocket, coral lace, or any of your machine-embroidery stitching. Pin every 4", working from the center out to the edges.

6. Turn the tapestry over to make sure the backing is smooth.

machine quilting practice

As with machine embroidery, it's a good idea to practice quilting on test samples before you quilt your tapestry. As you practice, adjust the tension as necessary.

1. Make 2 test "sandwiches," each 3" x 8", from your scraps of tapestry fabrics and fleece. Layer a piece of the tapestry background fabric on top of a layer of fleece and a scrap of the backing fabric.

2. Thread the top of the machine with invisible nylon thread. Use basting thread that matches the backing fabric in the bobbin.

3. Insert a new 80/12 (or 90/14, if your fabrics are heavy) needle.

4. Insert a free-motion embroidery foot.

5. Lower the feed dogs.

6. The straight-stitch length is determined by the speed in which you move as you quilt. Try to move the sandwich at a constant speed that is comfortable for you.

7. If your machine has a speed-control switch, set it for a slower speed.

8. When you begin machine quilting, always remember to set the stitch length at 0, draw the bobbin thread to the top, and take a few stitches to knot the threads. Clip thread tails.

9. Stitch through all layers, going from one end of the sample to the other.

10. Remove the sample from the machine and examine the stitches. If there are loops on the back side, increase (tighten) the top tension. If there are loops showing on the top, reduce (loosen) the top tension. Adjust by one number, sew, then adjust again if necessary.

11. Use your second test sandwich to practice your machine quilting. You want to be able to stitch continuously so that your stitches are the same length and so that you have smooth, curved lines. Remember, the more you practice, the better your stitching will be and the more confidence you will have!

TIPS FOR QUILTING

✦   Practice the stitching pattern you plan to use on your tapestry. Often, I follow the fabric's printed design. If the fabric has little or no print, I create a wave or stipple pattern. Refer to the quilting designs on pages 87–88.

✦   If you are not confident about quilting a design as you sew, mark a design on your tapestry first. Always test markers on scraps of your tapestry fabrics, to make sure the markings can be easily removed.

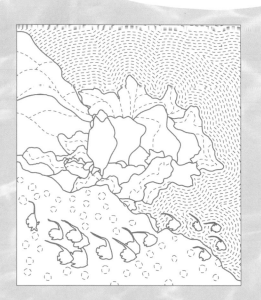

In the "Ocean Surgeonfish" tapestry, I used the stipple pattern to add the illusion of movement in the water.

In the "Andaman Island" tapestry, I created depth and contrast by varying the stitching patterns. In the open areas of the background, the rows of stitching are about ¼" apart. The foreground fabric has circles printed on it, so I simply stitched around the circles. I outlined the fish to make them stand out more.

quilting your tapestry

The difference between quilting your practice samples and your tapestry is the size that you are working with. Read the following steps before stitching:

1. Begin stitching in the top left-hand corner, with the rolled side to your left. Stitch from the top left to the top right. When you are within 1" or so of a safety pin, insert the needle into the tapestry, then remove the pin.

2. Relax! You want fluid, steady movement so that your stitches are the same length and the quilting lines have smooth curves.

3. Place your hands on each side of the embroidery foot to keep the tapestry flat as you stitch.

4. Do not quilt over the satin-stitched edges of the appliquéd pieces, fish, sponge, sponge pocket, or lace coral.

5. After your tapestry is quilted, remove it from the machine and trim any loose threads.

6. To "square up" the edges of the fleece and backing, measure the left and right side edges to make sure they are equal. Trim as necessary, using a rotary cutter and ruler. Repeat with the top and bottom edges. *Do not* trim the edges of the tapestry top.

adding the borders

I like borders that also serve as bindings. Because of the textures and thickness of the fabrics that I use, I make straight corners rather than mitered corners. Make yours as I have, or do it the way you prefer.

I chose black velvet for the left side and bottom borders. For the other two sides, I used a fabric similar to, but lighter in color than the background, and I covered it with tulle. Cut all borders from the lengthwise or crosswise grain of the fabric—be consistent.

> **TIP:** To add a layer of tulle to a border, cut the fabric and tulle the same width, then stitch the two layers together along the long sides, $\frac{1}{4}$" inside the raw edges. Treat the resulting border strip as one fabric.

machine setup

1. Insert an even-feed (walking) foot.

2. Insert a new size 80/12 needle.

3. Thread the top of the machine with standard sewing thread. Use the same thread in the bobbin.

4. Reset the top and bobbin tensions to the normal tension settings. Set the stitch length to medium-length stitches.

5. Make sure the feed dogs are *up*.

determining border width

1. If the edges of the tapestry are uneven, measure the distance from the outside edge of the fleece to the outside edge of the tapestry at the point where the distance is greatest. Note the measurement.

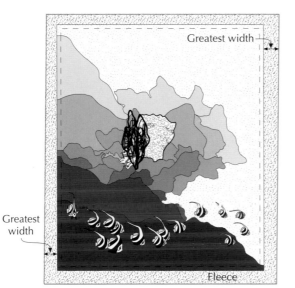

2. Mark a line on all sides of the tapestry top as shown, using the measurement from step 1. This line will be a guide for adding the borders.

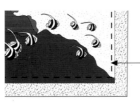

Mark a line around the tapestry top, using the measurement from step 1 above.

3. Calculate the finished width for the borders. Add ³⁄₈" for the seam allowance to the measurement that you noted in step 1. Note the measurement. If you want a narrower border, trim the fleece and backing to the desired width.

4. To calculate the width to cut the border strips, multiply by 2 the finished width that you noted in step 3.

cutting and stitching borders

Use ³⁄₈"-wide seam allowances, unless otherwise noted.

RIGHT SIDE BORDER

1. Cut one strip each from the background fabric and tulle to match the measurement of the width noted in step 4 above and 1" shorter in length than the length of the right edge of the fleece. Stitch the tulle strip to the fabric strip, following the directions in the Tip on page 63.

2. Press under ³⁄₈" on one long edge of the border strip.

3. With right sides together, place the border strip on top of the tapestry, aligning the long unturned edge of the border strip with the marked guideline (marked in step 2 of "Determining Border Width"). Align the top edge of the border strip ¹⁄₂" from the top edge of the fleece. Pin in place. Stitch.

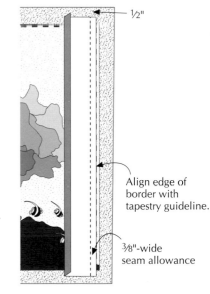

½"

Align edge of border with tapestry guideline.

³⁄₈"-wide seam allowance

4. Fold the strip to the back of the tapestry, along the edge of the fleece.

5. Slipstitch the border to the backing.

TOP BORDER

1. Cut one strip each from the background fabric and tulle. The length should match the width of the outer edge of the fleece, on the top of the tapestry. The width of the strips should match the measurement noted in step 4 of "Determining Border Width."

2. Press under $^3/_8$" on one long edge of the border strip.

3. With right sides together, place the border strip on top of the tapestry, aligning the long unturned edge of the border strip with the marked guideline (marked in step 2 of "Determining Border Width"). Align the left edge of the border strip $^1/_2$" from the left edge of the fleece. The border will extend $^1/_2$" beyond the finished edge of the right border. Pin in place. Stitch.

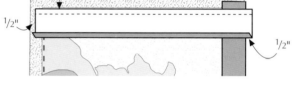

Align edge of border with tapestry guideline.

$^1/_2$" $^1/_2$"

4. Fold the border right sides together, even with the top edge of the fleece. Stitch the end seam, using a $^1/_2$"-wide seam allowance.

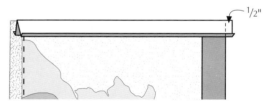

$^1/_2$"

5. Trim the seam and turn right side out. Fold the fabric over the fleece to the back side of the tapestry.

6. Slipstitch the border to the backing.

LEFT SIDE BORDER

1. From black velvet, cut a border strip that is the same length as the length of the outside

edge of the fleece on the left side of the tapestry. The width of the strip was noted in step 4 of "Determining Border Width."

2. Press under $^3/_8$" on one long edge of the border strip.

3. With right sides together, place the border strip on top of the tapestry, aligning the long unturned edge of the border strip with the marked guideline (marked in step 2 of "Determining Border Width"). Align the top edge of the border strip $^1/_2$" from the top edge of the fleece. Pin in place. Stitch.

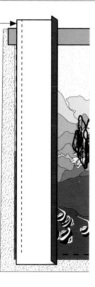

$^1/_2$"

4. Fold the border right sides together, even with the top edge of the fleece. Stitch the end seam, using a $^1/_2$"-wide seam allowance.

5. Trim the seam and turn right side out. Fold the fabric over the fleece.

6. Slipstitch the border to the backing.

BOTTOM BORDER

1. Cut a strip from the black velvet. The length of the strip should be 1" longer than the width of the fleece along the bottom edge of the tapestry. The width of the strip should match the measurement noted in step 4 of "Determining Border Width."

2. Press under $^3/_8$" on one long edge of the border strip.

3. With right sides together, place the border strip on top of the tapestry, aligning the long unturned edge of the border strip with the marked guideline (marked in step 2 of "Determining Border Width"). The border strip will extend ¹⁄₂" beyond the right and left side borders. Pin in place. Stitch.

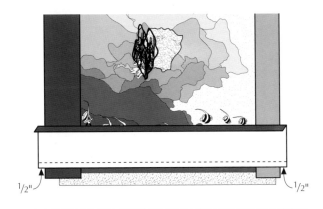

4. Fold the border right sides together, even with the lower edge of the fleece. Stitch the end seams, using a ¹⁄₂"-wide seam allowance.

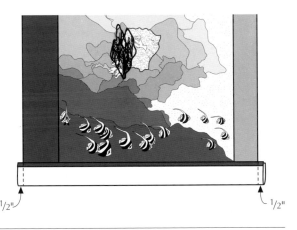

5. Trim the seams and turn right side out. Fold the fabric over the fleece and slipstitch.

adding a hanging sleeve

If you plan to hang your tapestry on a wall to display it, add a hanging sleeve. The finished sleeve width is 3", a standard size for quilt show entries.

1. Measure the finished width of your tapestry. From a sturdy piece of fabric, such as home-decorating fabric, cut a 7"-wide strip. The length should be 2" less than the finished width of the tapestry.

2. With right sides together, stitch the long sides together, using a ¹⁄₂"-wide seam allowance. Turn the sleeve right side out. Press the sleeve so that the seam is centered on the back.

3. Hem the ends by turning under ¹⁄₄", then ¹⁄₄" again. Stitch close to the folded edge.

4. Centering the sleeve on the back of the tapestry, place it, seam side down, ¹⁄₂" from the top edge.

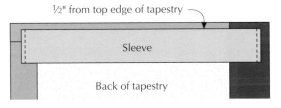

½" from top edge of tapestry

Sleeve

Back of tapestry

5. Slipstitch the top edge of the sleeve to the back of the tapestry. Make sure that your stitches do not go through to the front of the tapestry.

6. Raise the lower edge of the sleeve about ¹⁄₂" to create some give for the hanging rod and so the hanging rod does not put strain on the quilt. Slipstitch the sleeve's lower edge in place.

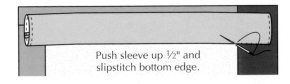

Push sleeve up ½" and slipstitch bottom edge.

ANDAMAN ISLAND [27" x 31"]

This group of islands lies south of Burma and west of Thailand. An incredible story of divers traveling to explore new territory prompted me to create this tapestry. I, too, wanted to explore new territory and push myself into new waters. The school of fish are members of the butterfly fish family and are common in Indo-Pacific waters. The dark fabric represents the boulder-strewn valleys in the Andaman Sea. Above the boulders, the coral flourish, supporting sponges and lace coral.

Adapting machine embroidery to clothing

Machine embroidery is an embellishment that individualizes a garment. My first attempt at embellishing was to embroider roses on a dress I made for my grandmother. She felt special knowing her dress was unique. We all see so much of the same thing when we walk into a department store. A bit of embroidery or appliqué adds creative expression to a garment and makes it uniquely our own.

I received an unusual pair of feather-shaped earrings from my husband. I discovered that I really didn't have anything that showed them off properly. So, I decided to make a special blouse to wear with them. I wanted to have a feather on the front of the blouse and on each cuff. I sketched the earring, then enlarged the design. With chalk, I drew the blouse pattern pieces onto fabric, then drew the feather design onto the fabric. I draped the fabric over myself and studied the effect in a mirror. By doing this, I was able to change the design and revise the placement of it before it was too late.

When you plan a design, take into consideration where the design will fall on your body. If you are using a pattern that you have never used before, take the time to work out the design before you cut the fabric. Once you are happy with your design, cut out the fabric pieces.

I added medium-weight, nonfusible, woven interfacing to the cuffs and collar, then backed them with tear-away stabilizer before I embroidered them. I always make a practice piece before stitching the design onto garment pieces. I layer a scrap of the garment fabric with interfacing and a layer of stabilizer.

I also experiment with different threads on practice pieces. For my "feather" blouse, I chose a shiny rayon thread to create a high contrast for the black and white lines, and a cotton thread in soft purple and blue colors.

Stitching the design was easy because the lines are all straight. Train your eyes to notice great designs and adapt them to your clothing!

When I first became interested in fish as a design theme, I created the sweatshirt shown on this page. The actual appliqué is simple; the cut of the yoke and its continuity is what makes the design work. I began by drawing the fish on paper, cutting out the shapes, then placing them around the yoke. Once I was happy with the placement, I cut the fish out of fabric. I also added the wavy lines cut from fabric to connect them and to give the design movement. Again, the design is simple. Each fish is one piece with details such as eyes and fins stitched in. I used a silver metallic thread to make the fish stand out, then a variety of fine cotton threads to emphasize the waves. All four fabrics, including the fabric behind the fish and the waves, are the same print—just in different colors!

From the numerous art classes that I have taken over the years, I will always remember one tip: draw what you know, and if you don't know, research the subject! Chose a subject that you are interested in or a design that you find attractive or exciting. The beautiful colors of fish first attracted me, and once I read about their habits, I became even more excited and eager to use them in my work.

Collect drawings and photos that appeal to you. I have files of photographs and articles that I use for my artwork. The files are divided into categories, such as sky scenes, horses, and birds. So, if I have the urge to design birds, there is usually an item in my folder to inspire me.

So many people think they cannot draw. If you fall into this group, think of drawing as composing and arranging. Try cutting out things, using a copy machine to enlarge or reduce images, and arrange them into a design that appeals to you. Start with something simple, such as decorating a pocket or collar. The results will spur you on to do more!

Trumpet vine vest

I designed the embellishments for this vest to help get you started. Use the vest pattern of your choice (I like Simplicity #9152 and McCalls #7173) and the appliqué designs that I have included, or improvise and use your own designs!

These appliqué designs are stitched to the vest in three sections. The first section is on the right front and wraps over the shoulder to the back. The area from the left side seam up to and including the hummingbird constitutes the second section. The third section includes the area covering the left shoulder, front and back.

Choose fabric in a light color for the vest. The greens and oranges of the appliqué design will be more prominent against a light color. For the lining, I chose a predominantly blue print that looks like large feathers!

The appliqué templates are on pages 91–95. Note that they are already reversed and ready to be traced. Refer to the Appliqué Placement Guides on pages 71–73 for placement of the pieces.

- ◆ Vest pattern of your choice (with lining and ⅝"-wide seam allowances)
- ◆ Fabrics and notions required by your pattern
- ◆ ¼ yd. fabric for leaves and stamens*
- ◆ 12" x 12" piece of vibrant-colored fabric for flowers
- ◆ 10" x 10" piece of fabric for hummingbirds**
- ◆ 1 yd. paper-backed fusible web, such as Wonder-Under or HeatnBond
- ◆ 1 yd. tear-away stabilizer
- ◆ Embroidery threads to complement your fabrics
- ◆ Basting thread, such as Brooks basting thread by J. & P. Coats
- ◆ Size 75/11 or 80/12 machine-embroidery needles
- ◆ Sharp embroidery scissors
- ◆ Pencil

Choose a fabric in an abstract pattern that includes more than one shade of green. Tightly woven fabrics are easier to machine embroider because they do not fray or stretch as you sew.

**I chose a fabric that reminded me of bird feathers. You have the option to construct the birds in sections. Use solid colors and add stitching to represent feathers.*

making the vest

1. Following your pattern's directions, cut out the vest from your fabric.

2. With right sides together, sew the shoulder seams. Press seams open.

> TIP: Appliqué the leaves and flowers in numerical order as indicated on the templates. Do not be concerned about aligning the appliqué pieces with the grain line of the fabrics—the effects of the colors and pattern of the print are what is important!

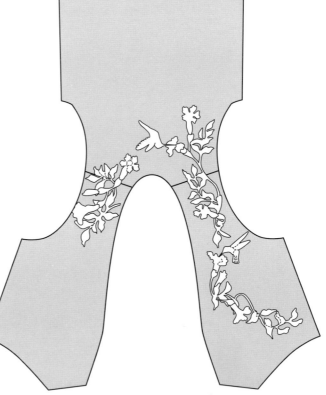

Appliqué Placement Guide

section one

Refer to the Appliqué Placement Guide for Section One.

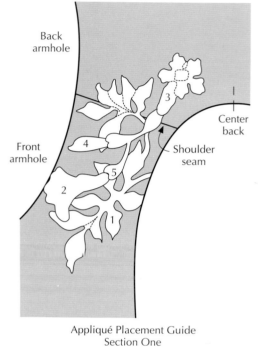

Back armhole

Front armhole

3

Center back

4

Shoulder seam

5

2

1

Appliqué Placement Guide
Section One

1. Trace the appliqué designs (Templates 1–5) onto the paper side of fusible web with pencil.

2. Fuse the web pieces to the wrong sides of your appliqué fabrics. Cut out each piece on the pencil line. Remove the backing paper.

3. Pin appliqué piece 1 to the vest. Fuse in place.

4. Repeat step 3 for appliqué pieces 2–5. Note that the stamen (piece 5) covers the lower edge of the flower and bud.

section two

Refer to the Appliqué Placement Guide for Section Two.

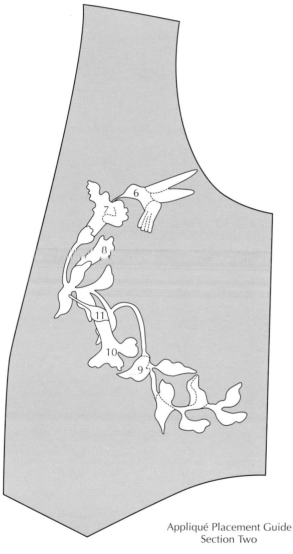

6

7

8

11

10

9

Appliqué Placement Guide
Section Two

1. Make your hummingbird in one piece and add stitching to delineate feather lines; or cut it in sections. If you want to appliqué the bird in sections, follow steps 2–6 below. If you cut your bird out in one piece, fuse it in place as you did for the appliqué pieces in Section One.

2. If your bird fabric has distinct lines that you want to use to represent feather lines, mark the lines from the templates onto the paper backing of fusible web. Trim around the shape, adding about ¼" all around.

3. Tape the fabric to a window with the wrong side of the fabric facing you. Beginning with piece 6A, place the fusible piece over the fabric and align it with the fabric. Pin in place.

4. Fuse the web to the wrong side of the bird fabric.

5. Repeat with pieces 6B–6E. Remove the backing paper from each piece.

6. Fuse the pieces in place on the vest in numerical order.

7. Prepare pieces 7–11 and fuse them to the vest in numerical order as you did with the other appliqué pieces. Note that leaves cover a portion of the lower edges of a flower (piece 7) and a bud (piece 11).

Refer to the Appliqué Placement Guide for Section Three.

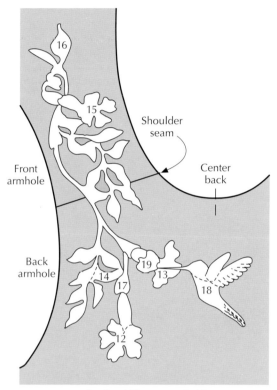

Appliqué Placement Guide
Section Three

Prepare pieces 12–19 and fuse them to the vest in numerical order as you did with the other appliqué pieces. Note that piece 15 partially covers some of the leaves and that an extra petal 19, lies on top of flower piece 13.

machine embroidery

Review the section on machine embroidery, beginning on page 20. Follow the instructions on machine setup. Insert a free-motion embroidery foot and a new size 75/11 or 80/12 embroidery needle.

1. Pin tear-away stabilizer behind the vest areas that have appliqué.

2. Using the practice leaf below, trace the design onto a scrap of fusible web. Fuse it to a scrap of your leaf fabric and cut out the piece.

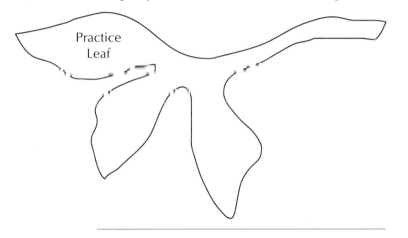

Practice
Leaf

3. Fuse the practice leaf to a scrap of your vest fabric. Pin or baste tear-away stabilizer on the wrong side of the vest fabric.

4. Thread the top of your machine with embroidery thread. Use basting thread in the bobbin. Set the zigzag stitch width to medium.

5. Starting at the top of the stem, move at a constant, comfortable speed. You can completely cover the edge by using a shorter stitch length (such as a satin stitch) or have a more open stitch.

6. The tips of the leaves will take a little practice. You can taper the points by narrowing the stitch width as you approach the point.

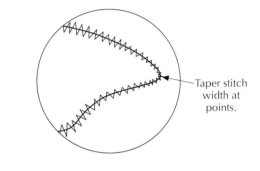

Taper stitch width at points.

7. Another way of stitching the points is to place the needle in the fabric at the outside edge of the point and pivot by raising the presser foot and turning the fabric. Lower the presser foot and resume stitching. Note that your new stitches will cover some of the previous stitches.

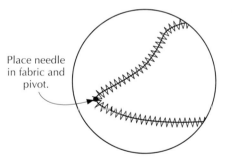

Place needle in fabric and pivot.

8. After completing the sample, you should have the confidence you need to work on your vest. If you are still a bit unsure, take the time to practice some more.

stitching the appliqués on the vest

1. Refer to the templates and draw the dashed lines onto your appliqués. These are additional stitching lines that help to define the detail of the flowers and leaves.

2. I used a variety of green and blue threads around the leaves to give the leaves shading. Vary your colors or use variegated thread to achieve depth. Be brave and try some of the techniques in "Design Ideas to Try" on pages 47–48).

3. Begin stitching around the outside edges of the leaves in Section One, near the front at the neck edge. When you come to a flower, stitch up its edge, then knot the thread. Clip only the top thread, then move the fabric to the nearest leaf and continue stitching.

4. The additional stitching lines (to define details) are stitched in the same manner as the outlining. Use the same thread and the same stitch width.

5. Stitch all of the leaves and stamens in Sections Two and Three.

6. Stitch the flowers and buds in all three sections. I chose a variegated thread that helps define the flowers.

7. The stitching lines on the hummingbirds are the same whether you have appliquéd them in one piece or in sections. Again, vary the thread color to create depth.

8. Trim all threads and remove all tear-away stabilizer.

9. Press the vest on the wrong side.

NOTE: Do not stitch the sides of the vest or vest lining until later!

finishing the vest

1. Follow the pattern directions for cutting out the lining.

2. Sew the lining fronts to the lining back at the shoulder seams. Press the seams open.

3. Lay the appliquéd vest right side up on a flat surface. Place the tissue pattern pieces over the vest and pin in place. Sometimes the appliqué stitching may draw up the fabric. This will most likely happen in the greatest area of stitching, the left front.

4. Check both front pieces and the back. On the wrong side of the vest fabric, mark the stitching line wherever the seam allowance is less than ⅝", so you will have a stitching guide in those places. It is not necessary to mark the areas where the tissue edges match the edges of the vest.

If vest is smaller than tissue pattern, mark where seam allowance is less than ⅝" and sew accordingly.

5. Place the vest and vest lining right sides together. Pin, matching the marked stitching lines of the vest with the ⅝"-wide seam allowance of the lining.

6. Starting at the center back neck edge, stitch the lining to the vest around the neck, down the front, then along the bottom edge to side seam as shown, using a ⅝"-wide seam allowance.

7. Starting at the center back neck edge, go around the other outer edge.

8. Stitch the vest and lining together along the bottom edge of the back of the vest. Start in the center and stitch to one of the side seams. Repeat, stitching to the remaining side seam.

9. Starting at the shoulder seam, stitch to the front side seam; then stitch from the shoulder seam to the back side seam.

10. Do the same on the other armhole.

11. Trim the seams to ¼".

12. Turn the vest right side out and press.

13. With right sides together and raw edges aligned, pin the vest front to the back at the side seams, matching the armhole and lower edge seam lines. Starting on the lining 1" above the armhole seam, stitch the vest side seams together, ending the stitching on the lining 1" below the seam at the bottom edge of the vest.

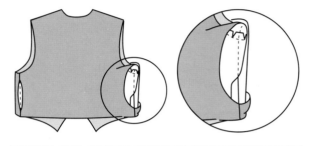

14. Press side seams toward the vest back. Turn right side out and press again. Turn under the side seam allowances on the lining back and blindstitch to the lining front along the side seam allowance.

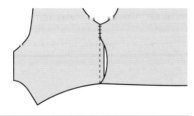

15. If your vest has buttons, follow your pattern directions for making buttonholes. Sew on buttons.

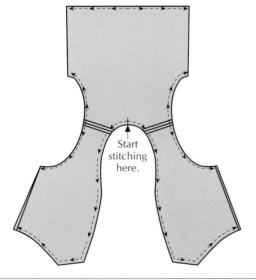

Start stitching here.

TRUMPET VINE VEST

This hearty vine grows wild where I live. It tends to wrap itself around pine trees, blooming high in the trees. You know the vine is there when the brightly colored flowers fall to the ground. I watched hummingbirds feeding on the nectar of the trumpet vine flowers in my backyard. The slender bill of the hummingbird fits perfectly in the long trumpet blossom.

fterword

Nothing is as frustrating or as rewarding as creating a new piece of artwork. With each piece, I want to learn new things by experimenting with design and fabric techniques. My process involves learning a new technique, practicing it until I know it, then experimenting and taking it a step further. Each tapestry allows me the freedom to find another way to visualize the environment of the sea and the habitats of fish. I strive not to make the next piece better, but different and personally challenging.

Long ago, I quit the inner battle of asking myself how many hours I had in a tapestry. Now I continue working on a tapestry until I am satisfied. A few compositions have left me puzzled and will sit for awhile until I have an answer or a clue as to the next step to take. For this reason, I keep two or three pieces going at the same time. At times, I test out a variety of ideas until one works.

Creating art means taking risks and, with each work, expecting more of myself. Do not be disillusioned, thinking "this is easy for you, but hard for me." Learning, trying—and yes, ripping out—are necessary ingredients for each piece of artwork. Be willing to jump in and try something new. Refuse to give up, and you will be successful! I do a lot of experimenting and I encourage you to do the same!

meet the author

The urge to create has always been inside Ginny. As a child, she loved to color and draw. She made clothes for her Troll dolls and spent her spare time at the local hobby shop. When Ginny was nine and living in Mt. Healthy, Ohio, the mayor's wife taught her to sew a dress by hand! Ginny's grandmother, Hattie Gillivan, and mother loved to sew, and with Ginny's budding interest, they enrolled her in sewing classes. By the time she was in high school, Ginny looked at the latest styles in magazines and made them herself.

Ginny Eckley

Through high school, Ginny tried various arts and crafts, including crochet, weaving, and batik. Her love for sewing grew, and she majored in clothing and textiles in college. At the same time, she enrolled in every sewing class available, including classes in fiber sculpture and weaving. Upon completing several art courses, Ginny switched her major and ultimately graduated with a Fine Arts degree from the University of Houston in 1976.

After graduating, she worked with a designer making custom leather clothing and accessories. ZZ Top (the rock-and-roll band) was one of her clients! At the same time, Ginny took classes in art glass. Ever since, her art has alternated between sewing and glass. Through her glass commissions, she has had the pleasure of creating lamps, cabinet doors, entryways, and even a curved glass wall. Although fabric and glass seem worlds apart, each provides unique artistic opportunities.

Ginny lives in Kingwood, Texas, a suburb of Houston, with her husband, Ty, and two children, Amber and Forest. Thanks to Ty, she always has a studio.

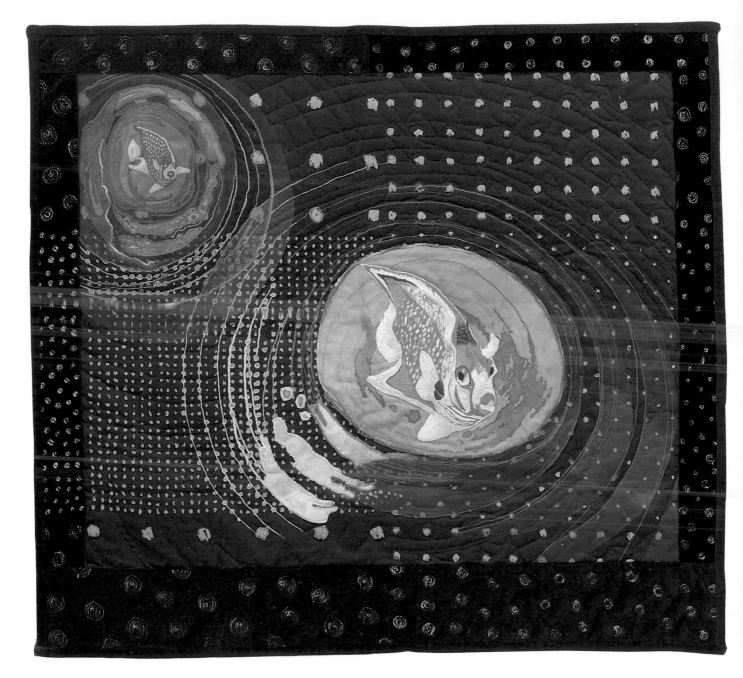

ATLANTIC QUEEN ANGELFISH [32" x 29"]

These exquisite fish go through many color changes as they mature. The Atlantic Queen Angelfish can be found on the tropical reefs of the Caribbean. Since they do not swim together in schools, I chose to show two of them, swimming fairly far apart, with only white specks glowing in the water. From the collection of David Eckley.

Practice Fish Pattern

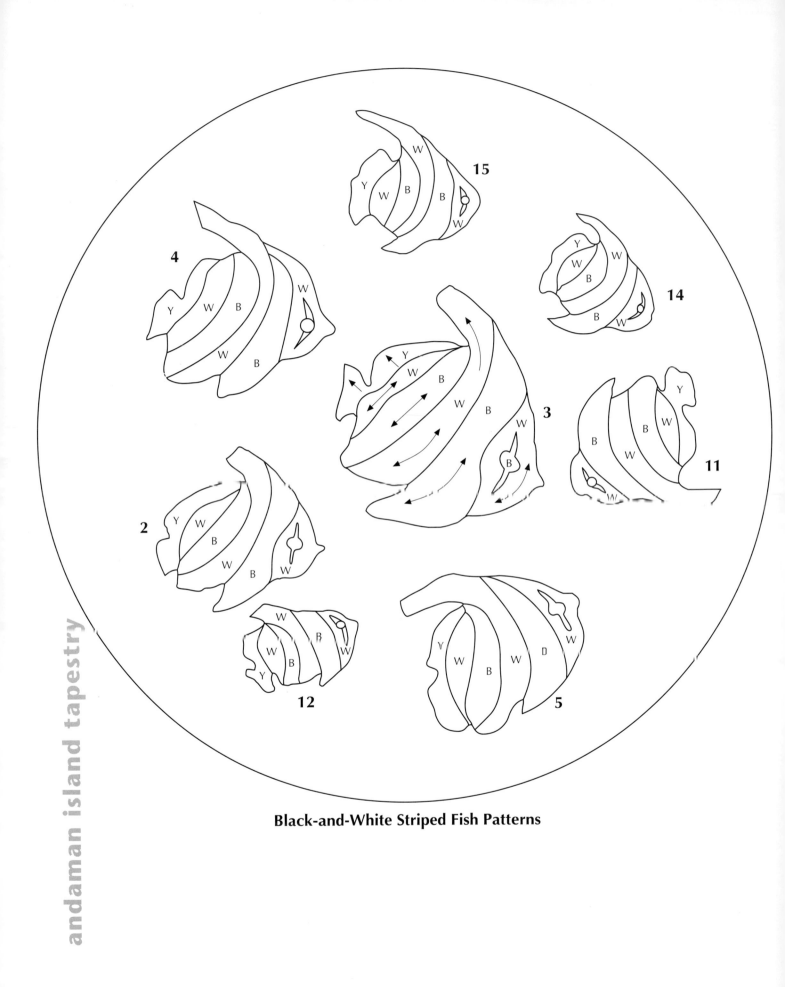

Black-and-White Striped Fish Patterns

Black-and-White Striped Fish Patterns

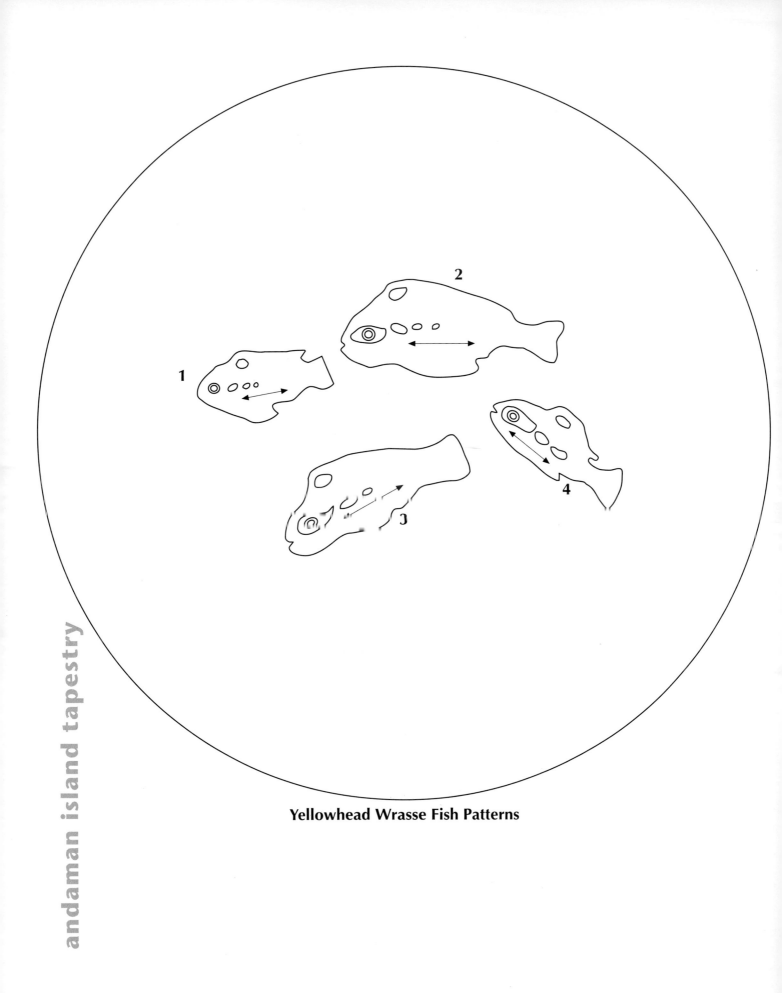

Yellowhead Wrasse Fish Patterns

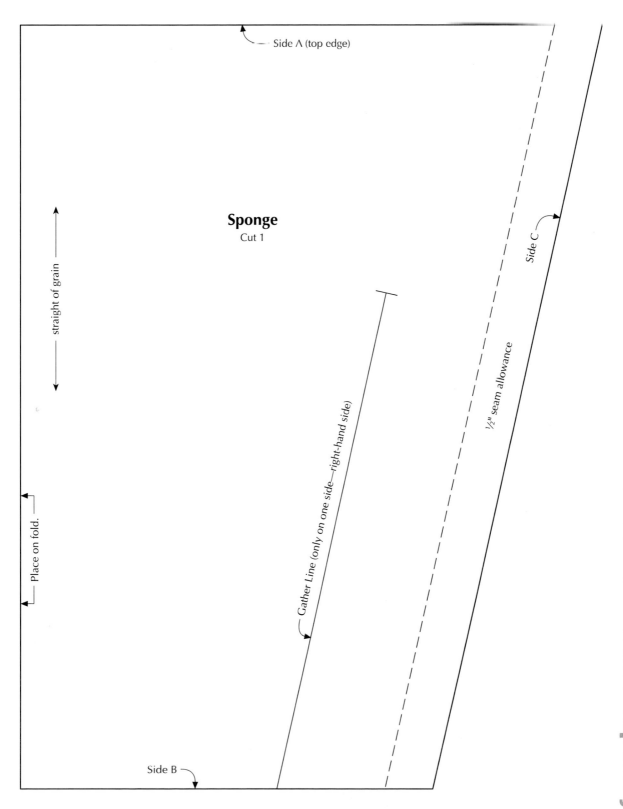

Sponge
Cut 1

Side A (top edge)

straight of grain

Place on fold.

Gather Line (only on one side—right-hand side)

½" seam allowance

Side C

Side B

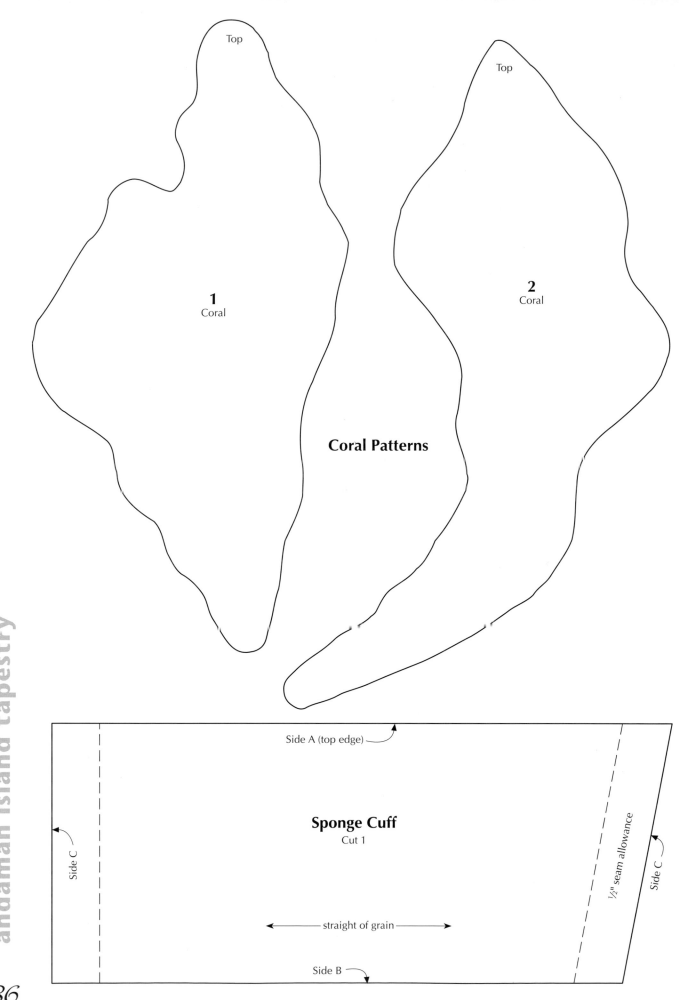

Top

1
Coral

Top

2
Coral

Coral Patterns

Side A (top edge)

Side C

½" seam allowance

Side C

Sponge Cuff
Cut 1

straight of grain

Side B

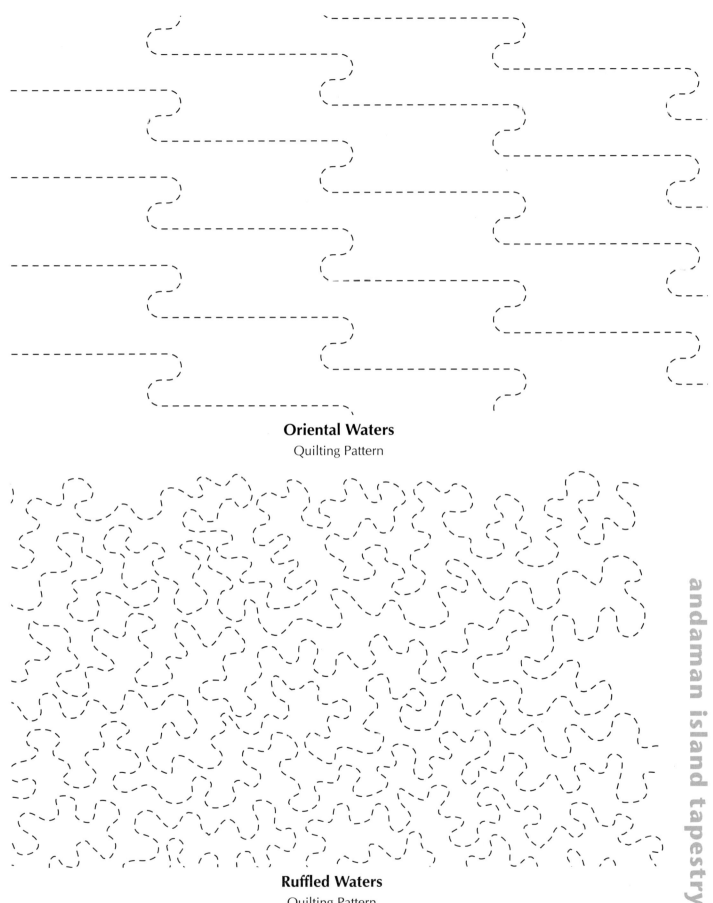

Oriental Waters
Quilting Pattern

Ruffled Waters
Quilting Pattern

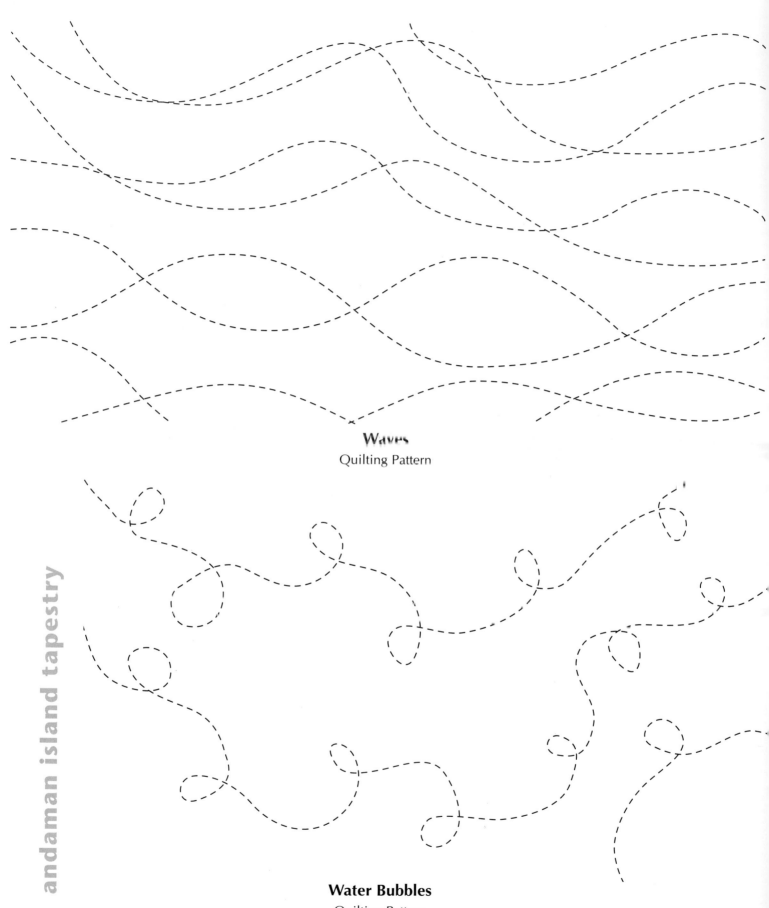

Waves
Quilting Pattern

Water Bubbles
Quilting Pattern

Andaman Island Tapestry
Template Seam Allowance Guide #1

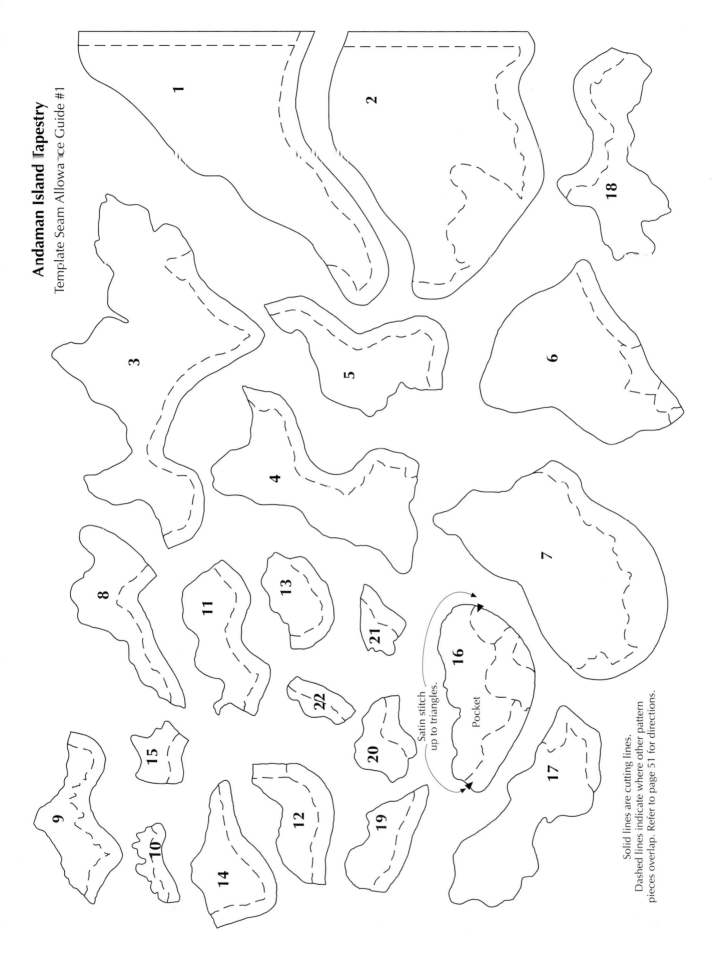

1

2

18

3

5

6

4

7

8

11

13

21

16

Pocket

Satin stitch
up to triangles.

22

20

17

9

15

10

14

12

19

Solid lines are cutting lines.
Dashed lines indicate where other pattern
pieces overlap. Refer to page 51 for directions.

89

Andaman Island Tapestry
Template Seam Allowance Guide #2

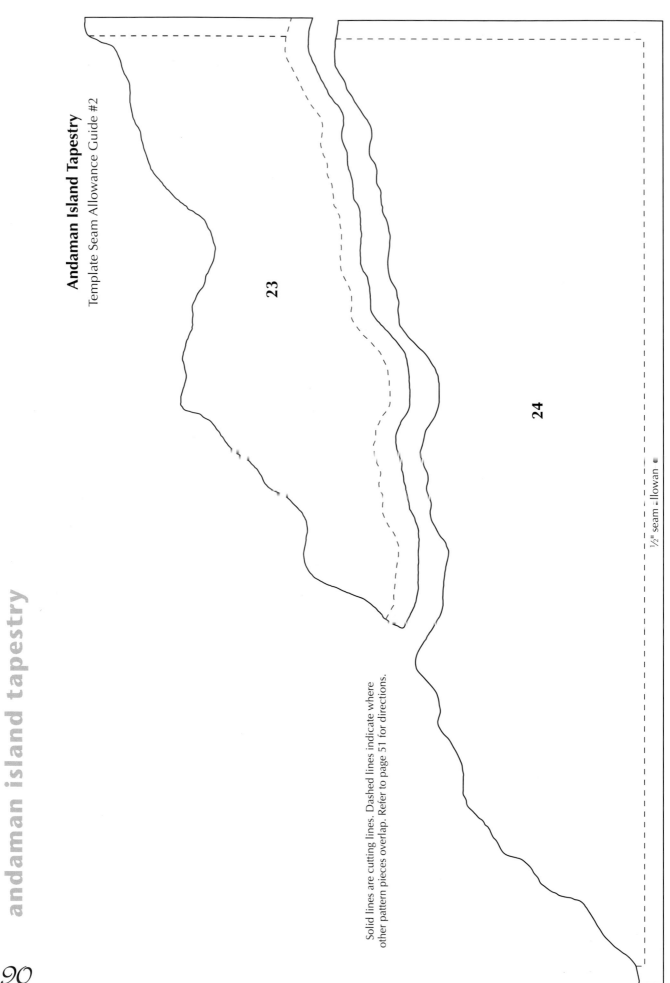

23

24

Solid lines are cutting lines. Dashed lines indicate where other pattern pieces overlap. Refer to page 51 for directions.

½" seam allowance

1
Cut 1

5
Cut 1

4
Cut 1

3
Cut 1

2
Cut 1

trumpet vine vest

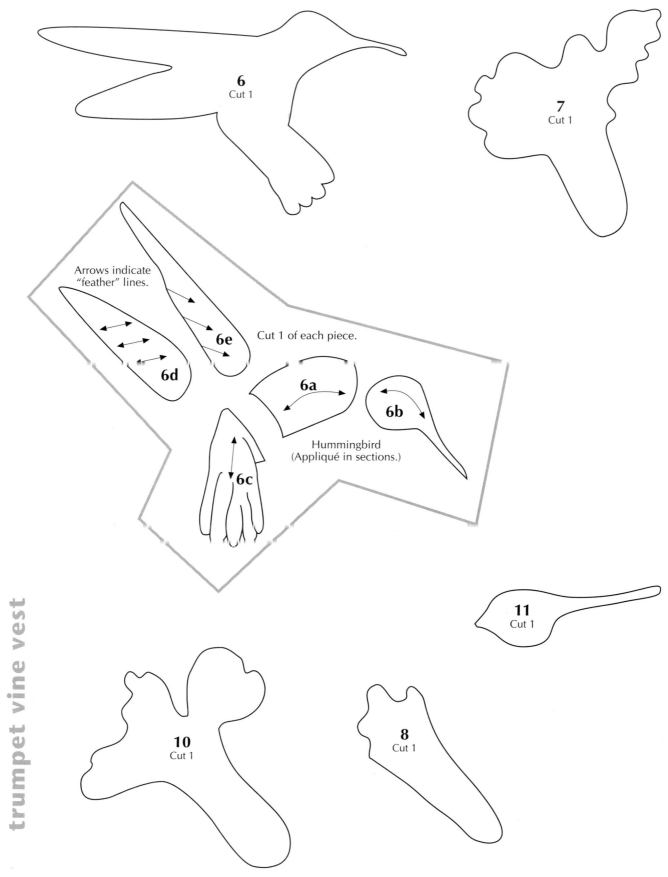

6
Cut 1

7
Cut 1

Arrows indicate
"feather" lines.

Cut 1 of each piece.

6e

6d

6a

6b

Hummingbird
(Appliqué in sections.)

6c

11
Cut 1

trumpet vine vest

10
Cut 1

8
Cut 1

9
Cut 1

trumpet vine vest

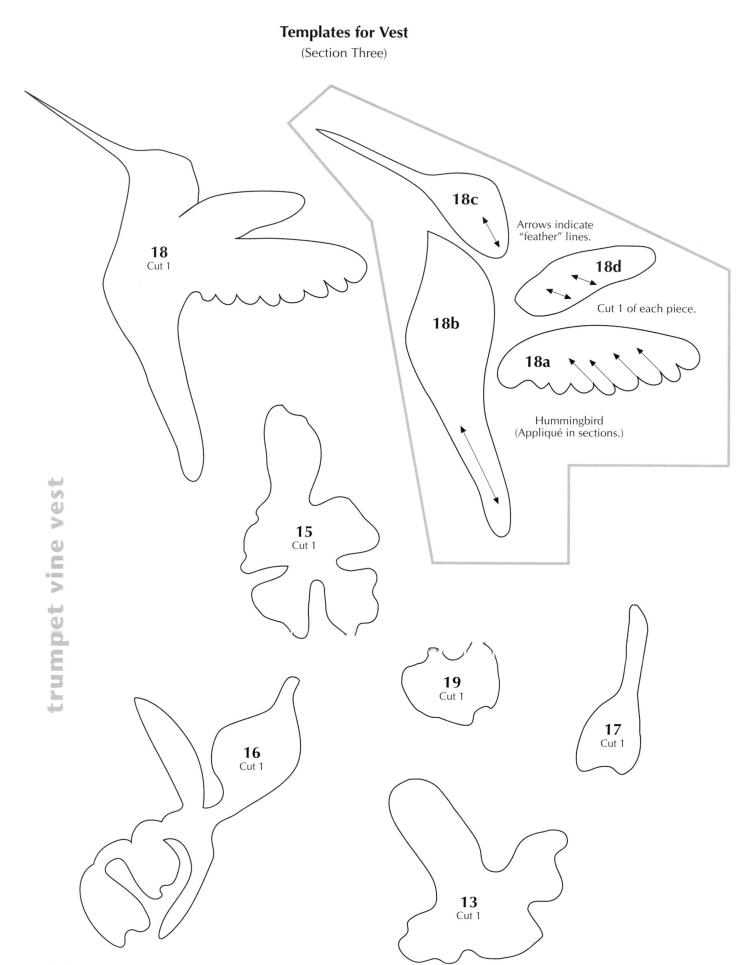

Templates for Vest
(Section Three)

18c

Arrows indicate "feather" lines.

18d

Cut 1 of each piece.

18a

Hummingbird
(Appliqué in sections.)

18
Cut 1

18b

trumpet vine vest

15
Cut 1

19
Cut 1

17
Cut 1

16
Cut 1

13
Cut 1

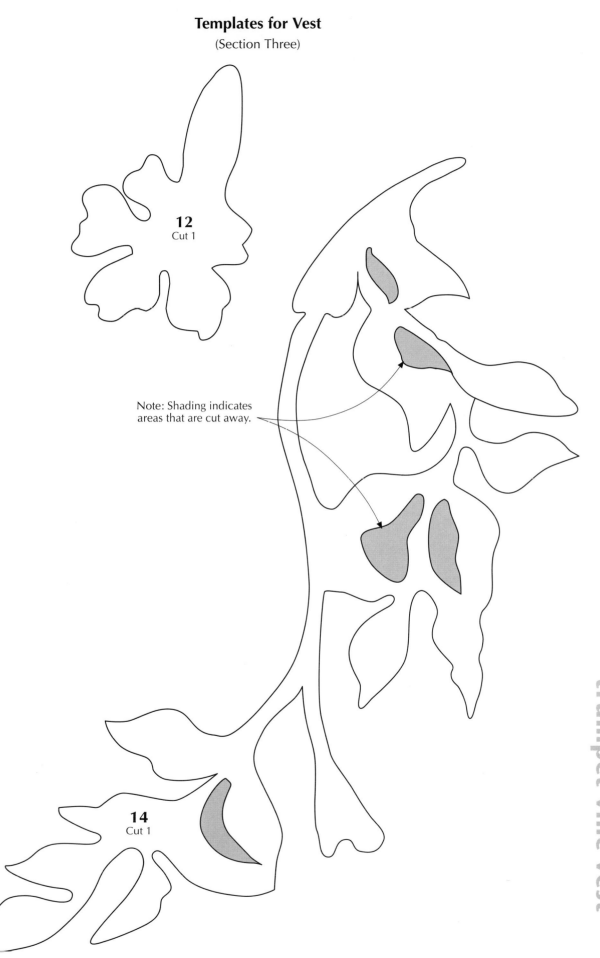

12
Cut 1

Note: Shading indicates
areas that are cut away.

14
Cut 1

That Patchwork Place Publications and Products